PSYCHOLOGY PRACTITIONER GUIDEBOOKS

EDITORS
Arnold P. Goldstein, Syracuse University
Leonard Krasner, Stanford University & SUNY at Stony Brook
Sol L. Garfield, Washington University in St. Louis

GESTALT THERAPY
Second Edition

Titles of Related Interest

Bornstein/Bornstein MARITAL THERAPY: A Behavioral-Communications Approach

Ellis/Sichel/Yeager/DiMattia/DiGiuseppe RATIONAL-EMOTIVE COUPLES THERAPY

Ellis/McInerney/DiGiuseppe/Yeager RATIONAL-EMOTIVE THERAPY WITH ALCOHOLICS AND SUBSTANCE ABUSERS

Garfield THE PRACTICE OF BRIEF PSYCHOTHERAPY

Golden/Dowd/Friedberg HYPNOTHERAPY: A Modern Approach

Lakin THE HELPING GROUP: Therapeutic Principles and Issues

Related Journal

CLINICAL PSYCHOLOGY REVIEW

GESTALT THERAPY
Practice and Theory
Second Edition

MARGARET P. KORB
Gestalt Center of Gainesville

JEFFREY GORRELL
Southeastern Louisiana University

VERNON VAN DE RIET
Affiliated Psychological Services of Southern California

ALLYN AND BACON
Boston London Toronto Sydney Tokyo Singapore

Printed in the United States of America

10 9 8 7 6 5 4 3 2   96 95 94 93 92

ISBN 0-205-14395-4

Library of Congress Cataloging in Publication Data

Korb, Margaret P., 1920-
  Gestalt therapy : practice and theory / Margaret P. Korb,
Jeffrey Gorrell, Vernon Van De Riet. -- 2nd ed.
    p.   cm. -- (Psychology practitioner guidebooks)
  Rev. ed. of: Gestalt therapy, an introduction / Vernon Van De
Riet, Margaret P. Korb., John Jeffrey Gorrell. c1980.
  Bibliography: p.
  Includes indexes.
    1. Gestalt therapy. I. Gorrell, John Jeffrey, 1945-   . II. Van
De Riet, Vernon, 1935-   . III. Van De Riet, Vernon, 1935-
Gestalt therapy, an introduction. IV. Title. V. Series.
  [DNLM: 1. Psychological Theory. 2. Psychotherapy. WM 420
K836g]
RC489.G4K67 1989
616.89'143--dc19
DNLM/DLC   89-2954
for Library of Congress   CIP

Contents

Preface to the Second Edition

The first edition of this book, titled *Gestalt Therapy: An Introduction*, was presented as an introductory level treatment of Gestalt therapy theory and practice. We saw our audience as students of clinical and counseling psychology, who wanted to know more about this particular therapy. Consequently, we took a fairly strong academic slant in the book, focusing on providing the groundwork and antecedents of the therapy as well as delineating practice, particularly in F. Perls' workshops. In this later edition, we have concentrated on providing a more practitioner-oriented treatment of Gestalt therapy, as well as attempting to reflect the important changes that have occurred in Gestalt therapy over the past decade. A person acquainted with the first edition will find that some discussions have been dropped from this edition, many topics have been revised to conform to contemporary thinking, and some new topics have been added. Before outlining the new features of this edition, we will spend a little time describing our conceptions of the changes that have been occurring during the 1980s and how those changes have influenced this edition.

In 1980, Gestalt therapy was emerging from a period in which Frederick S. Perls' writings and later therapy style had been dominant. Although many therapists were evolving their own styles and were adding needed elaborations and refinements to Gestalt theory, the strong tendency was for therapists and theorists alike to look to Fritz Perls' work for the final work on any particular topic. Our book reflected that orientation, from its inception through its publication. A quick look at the earlier edition will reveal copious references to F. Perls, as opposed to references to Gestalt therapy in its more general framework, and numerous quotations from F. Perls.

While this leaning toward F. Perls was appropriate for those times, and while it adequately reflected the impact that F. Perls had on the early and later development of Gestalt therapy, the intervening years since 1980 have shown that the history and theory of Gestalt therapy is more complex and involves more individuals than was indicated at that time. At the time we wrote the first version of this book—during the late 70s—Gestalt therapy was still thought of as conforming to F. Perls' "workshop" style of the late 60s, during which time he presented dramatic demonstrations of various Gestalt techniques using dreamwork, the hot seat, and various other expressive techniques. The films in which F. Perls appeared were, for many therapists, the only contact with him outside his books.

F. Perls' books from the 60s and early 70s also tended to reflect the dramatic and confrontative orientation of their writer. The more dense and theoretically more complete *Gestalt Therapy* (F. Perls, Hefferline, & Goodman, 1951) from earlier days was read by only the most avid. F. Perls found an audience for Gestalt therapy in the 60s that appreciated a more personal and "freewheeling" descriptive style than appeared in the early writings. Additionally, the humanistic psychology movements of the 60s led to the development of growth centers such as Esalen and the popularization of encounter groups, as well as many other types of growth groups. Gestalt therapy became linked in many people's minds with the excesses of those attempts to break out of conventional modes of expression and interaction. Because of this association, the more rigorous and dedicated Gestalt theorists were not heard as frequently; even among practicing therapists, there was this tendency to treat F. Perls' words and manner of therapy as gospel.

Erving Polster, reflecting, in 1987, in the tenth anniversary edition of *The Gestalt Journal*, on the many distortions of Gestalt therapy based on an overreliance on later F. Perls commentary and built upon a noncritical orientation of therapists, says,

> Indispensable words,—it, we, why, but, and others—were stereotypically thought to be excluded from the Gestalt lexicon. The empty chair turned into the ubiquitous chair, anger was taken as evidence of honesty, the here-and-now exalted amnesia, self support became an excuse for isolation, etc. In short, we as Gestalt therapists, often became identified with burlesques of our principles, with no more possibilites of clarification than is available in any spread of rumor (1987, p.34).

Over the last 15 years, Laura Perls, Erving and Miriam Polster, Gary Yontef, Joe Wysong, Joel Latner, Jack Aylward, Robert Resnick, Joseph Zinker, and many others have contributed mightily to furthering Gestalt theory and practice. *The Gestalt Journal*, under the editorship of Joe Wysong, in fact celebrated its 10th anniversary in 1987, amply demonstrating that the 80s have been a time of resurgence and renewal in Gestalt theory. From the pages of *The Gestalt Journal* to the annual conferences on the theory and practice of Gestalt therapy, therapists and theorists have engaged in concentrated dialogue about basic issues in Gestalt therapy. Out of these discussions have grown more balanced understandings of the dynamics of change, the role of the therapist, and the nature of the individual.

Some major confrontations that have influenced the current state of Gestalt therapy have centered around the nature of the self—what it is, how it is distinguished from self-concept, and how therapy is affected by a process orientation toward the self. A major shift in understanding therapy has occurred as the limitations of an intrapersonal focus for therapy (therapist as observer or catalyst only) have been explored, leading, most notably from the writings of Polster and Polster, to incorporation of an interpersonal orientation (therapist as participant) in therapy, where contacts between client and the environment (including the therapist) are considered to be rich sources of awareness and change. Concerns over the limitations of Gestalt therapy, particularly F. Perls' workshop therapy, with narcissistic and borderline clients has also forced reconsideration of the roles of the therapist.

Because of the changes in our basic orientation, away from an academic treatment and toward a practitioner's treatment, and because of the changes in the field of Gestalt therapy itself, we, in this manuscript, have made changes in organization and labeling along with content changes that will be delineated in the following paragraphs.

In chapter 1, *The Foundations of Gestalt Therapy*, we have focused on providing a more coherent and detailed description of the particular principles of gestalt functioning, many of which current Gestalt theorists have been increasingly concentrating on. Gestalt principles have been expanded to include discussions of figure-ground, gestalt formation and completion, emergent needs, clarity of gestalten, awareness and attention, closure, and holism; some of these are either new or much revised discussions of traditionally important Gestalt topics. Additionally, an outline of Gestalt therapy principles and concepts is added to the chapter. These are the principles that are built upon in succeeding chapters, as we delve more deeply into the practice of Gestalt therapy. This has been done in order to provide the reader with a strong initial exposure to the theory on which discussions of subsequent Gestalt issues build.

Sections from the first edition have been removed from chapter 1. We no longer discuss the nature of theories, which now seems to be an unnecessary topic considering the new focus of this book. Likewise, a discussion of Gestalt therapy's relationship with Behaviorism has been deleted, and the section on therapy antecedents has been moved to chapter 4, renamed, and expanded to include relationships with other therapies.

The extensive discussions of philosophical assumptions that formed chapter 2 in the first edition have been deleted. A brief entry related to philosophical assumptions, however, has been added at the end of chapter 1. Readers who wish to examine the philosophical bases of Gestalt therapy in greater depth are referred to the first edition.

Chapter 2, *Psychodynamics*, is now organized around personality structure and personality dynamics. Under the topic of personality structure, an entirely new section on the gestalt-formation-completion cycle picks up the main idea of gestalt completion from chapter 1 and delineates, with a figure and extended examples, how this cycle occurs within the individual. This discussion sets the stage for further discussion of the process in chapter 5. New formulations regarding the self have led to new distinctions between self-as-concept and self-as-process, as well as the interaction of the two: these are presented in new sections of this chapter. Likewise, a prior discussion on the ego has been deleted, since ego is not stressed currently in Gestalt theory.

Under the heading of *Personality Dynamics*, updated discussions of contact and the I-boundary, reflecting the Polster and Polster contribution to theory on contact and boundaries, are included. The F. Perlsian way of describing contact has been enhanced by the addition of the Polsters' way. Other discussions—of the zones of experience, symbolization, contact-withdrawal, and identification-alienation—have remained essentially the same as in the first edition.

Chapter 3, besides reorganizing the discussion from before, provides new material on contactfulness, which is then related to standard topics, such as responsibility and boundary disturbances. Deflection is added to the discussion of boundary disturbances. Introjection and projection are now treated as companion processes instead of separate ones, and a new section on depression has been added to the discussion.

In chapter 4, new sections on the course of therapy, maturational steps, style in therapy, and stages of therapy are presented. A section on the course of therapy and maturational steps incorporates advanced principles related to how the individual grows (matures) through the therapeutic encounter. This discussion emphasizes the long-term changes that may occur, using extended examples, going beyond the tendency to talk of episodes in therapy, as if those episodes encapsulate the whole of therapy process.

The section on relationships with other therapies has retained a main discussion related to psychoanalytic therapies, but now includes mention of self-psychology, as well. There are new sections on cognitive, existential and phenomenological, and behavioral therapies, providing a balance not presented in the first edition.

Chapter 5 is an almost new chapter. While it contains sections from the prior edition related to therapy techniques, now referred to as "classic experiments," more emphasis is placed on the creative and on-going dialogic process of therapy. Effective interventions are described as being of three types: existential, experimental, and experiential. Interventional modes now include the participant-observer stance of the therapist. Likewise, there are new sections on interventional strategies, experiments with the I-boundary, and individual and group work. From this chapter, the reader should now attain a more rounded and complete understanding of the ways that Gestalt therapists work with clients in on-going therapy.

Chapter 6 updates concerns about the therapist and the various functions the therapist may serve within Gestalt therapy. New sections consider the therapist as an instrument of change and as an educator, reflecting again the more interactive orientation of Gestalt therapy over the earlier versions. A brief discussion about training and some potential sources for training rounds out the chapter.

In an *Afterward*, we report on the current trends, issues, and concerns within the Gestalt therapy community. We look ahead to where Gestalt therapy seems to be headed.

Finally, the *Appendix* has been expanded to include transcripts of two different types of therapy approaches within Gestalt. The first transcript, from the first edition, represents the therapist as catalyst working on intrapersonal issues. The second transcript, new to this edition, represents the interactionist or participant orientation that Gestalt therapy may also take. Notes concerning the course of the sessions are included to clarify the processes and interventions that occur in each session.

Acknowledgments

The authors would like to thank Suellyn Winkle and Earl W. Capron for reading and commenting on the revised manuscript. Their professional advice, extended freely and capably, enabled us to present a more cogent exposition of Gestalt therapy theory and practice. We also thank Sudeep Balain and Vanessa Falgoust for their dedication to detail and accuracy in transcribing, typing, and organizing the new and old material in this edition. That kind of work, often going unheralded, was indispensable during all phases of preparation of the manuscript.

Chapter 1

Theoretical Foundations of Gestalt Therapy

Gestalt therapy was named after the learning theory proposed by Gestalt psychologists.[1] According to Laura Perls (Rosenfeld, 1982), selection of the word *Gestalt* to describe the approach to therapy developed by Frederick S. ("Fritz") Perls, Laura Perls, and others meeting with them in New York City in the late 1940s, occurred after they rejected the original name existential therapy, because of its negative association in many people's minds with Jean Paul Sartre and nihilism.

Gestalt, as the name for this new therapy, links the early therapists with the organismic theory of Goldstein and the organizing principles of gestalt learning theory as a basis for describing the overall functioning of individuals. Kohler's (1973) research on insight, conducted in 1927, and Wertheimer's (1945) principles of productive thinking stress the importance of understanding the underlying structure of a problem for true learning to occur. The underlying structure or configuration of a situation is perceived as a total organization; thus, a meaningful gestalt is the individual's personal construction of meaning out of the available field of impressions.

Gestalt is a German word for a complete pattern or configuration; the term cannot be translated into English with a single word or phrase. For a description, three phenomena must be considered: a thing, its context or environment, and the relationship between them. We perceive something that constitutes a part of the reality of our world in terms of the context in which it occurs. For example, the color and texture of a rosebud in the context of a vase in a room are perceived

---

[1]In this book *Gestalt* is capitalized whenever it refers to Gestalt therapy, theory, and practice; *gestalt* is not capitalized when it is used in the context of gestalt learning theory or gestalt formation and completion processes. Hopefully, preserving a distinction between the two uses of the word will clarify the explanations for the reader.

1

differently from the same rosebud when its context is many other rosebuds on a bush in a garden. Our response is quite different to the rosebud in the two contexts. Although the rosebud is the focus, the gestalt of the rosebud depends on, and cannot be separated from, the environment in which it appears. The whole of the rosebud consists of the thing itself and of its relationship to the environment. In Gestalt therapy, we consider that the experienced whole (the gestalt) includes the thing itself (the figure) and its meaning, which derives from its relationship to the context (the ground).

The concept of gestalt also is related to creativity, since gestalt formation is a creative process, a process of creating a meaningful pattern or configuration. The individual perceives the world in terms of figure-ground relationships; the relationship between these two things is what stands out in that person's experience. It becomes important, then, for a person to be able to react appropriately to what emerges, to what surfaces in that set of relationships.

When someone becomes a Gestalt therapist, the person takes on a set of assumptions (noted in this chapter as *principles)* along with a body of practical interventions. All of the assumptions of Gestalt therapy become the background for understanding and working with clients. Even if the assumptions are not articulated, they are influential in terms of what is seen in the client. The basic assumptions insure that the ground is rich, fertile, and complex, containing many possibilities for exploring the client's experience. In this way, figure and ground relationships are just as true with respect to therapy processes as they are in any other area of a person's life. Part of the process of becoming a Gestalt therapist is the development of an appropriate set of background assumptions from which therapy interventions can be generated.

The last decade has seen a re-emergence of understandings of the basic texts and early formulations of Gestalt therapy. The original principles of gestalt formation and of contact have taken on greater prominence in the writings and thinking of Gestalt theorists. An appreciation of the principles from Gestalt learning theory and the ways they are integrated into all the essential Gestalt therapy processes is clearly the starting point for those who wish to truly understand the therapy in its most meaningful and most powerful form. Because it is so important that a Gestalt therapist understand and appreciate the underpinnings of the therapy, the opening chapter of this book is devoted to exposition of the primary principles and a brief statement of the philosophical assumptions of Gestalt therapy. To learn Gestalt therapy as a set of interventions without understanding the underlying processes from which the interventions emerge, is to miss the most important dimensions of the therapy. Therefore, the reader is encouraged to dwell carefully upon the first half of this book, instead of moving immediately into the latter half where one may find discussion of interventions and therapist-client relationships, as well as extended examples from therapy sessions. The reader is also encouraged to explore the original statements of Gestalt therapy in F. Perls, Hefferline, and Goodman's *Gestalt therapy: Excitement and growth in the human personality* (1951).

Gestalt therapy is intuitively appealing to many therapists, counselors, and other mental health professionals. Its theoretical foundations are related to various psychological and philosophical perspectives: psychoanalytic and neoanalytic theories, phenomenology, existential thought, Eastern philosophy, General Semantics, and many other sources. It presents a synthesis of the dynamics of psychological functioning that creates in many people an immediate, positive recognition of the powerful constructs and interventions at its core. The rapid growth of interest in Gestalt therapy in the late 1960s and the persisting interest of professionals and laymen today attest to its popularity and success as a therapy.

There now are many recognized approaches to the process of ongoing therapy with clients who present a wide variety of clinical symptoms. The validity of Gestalt therapy has been increasingly recognized by the mainstream of therapeutic enterprises. Chapters on Gestalt therapy routinely appear in texts on counseling or clinical theory, although they often are much abbreviated and inevitably distorted by attention to certain well-known Gestalt techniques without corresponding attention being paid to the actual underlying framework of the therapy and the real practice that derives from it. Although it is encouraging to see Gestalt therapy taken so seriously, there is the danger that it will be introjected by the therapeutic community in ways that do violence to its underlying theory. Recently, the editorial board of *The Gestalt Journal* expressed concerns over attempts by writers and textbook editors to circumscribe the whole of Gestalt therapy in one brief chapter (Brown, From, Latner, Miller, Polster, Polster, Rawle, Wysong, Yontef, and Zinker, 1988).

A central value in Gestalt therapy is the integrated wholeness of personality; within that wholeness there are elements, such as a theory of health, disease, and the dynamics of personality (Perls et al., 1951). Since theories attempt to provide broad, holistic explanations of reality, an individual well-versed in any particular theory tends to rely on that theory as a touchstone for understanding. This often leads to confusion over what is conceptualized; what values, beliefs, and prejudices a person has; and what is real. Many people mistake a theory for the truth; they do not see the theory merely as one possible way of organizing perceptions. It is not unusual for psychologists to act as if they believe that reinforcement, for example, is a real entity instead of only a useful explanatory concept. Others may believe that the id, ego, and super-ego exist, or that the self-concept is more than a person's own theory about herself or himself. Just as an individual may employ different problem-solving strategies, depending upon the particular goals that have been set, so may an individual rely upon different theories of behavior at different times. Thus, Gestalt therapy may be viewed as one possible way to understand human behavior, one many persons find useful in therapy, clinical work, counseling, and organizational development.

Many of the interventions created by Gestalt therapists are being used by therapists with other then Gestalt backgrounds (Rosenfeld, 1982). In fact, many of the Gestalt interventions coincide with interventions used in other therapies. Those interventions that are specifically part of the Gestalt therapy model, however, stand up well under the scrutiny of therapists from many different persuasions. In this chapter, we will discuss the major assumptions underlying the practice of Gestalt therapy, placing particular emphasis on principles and theories.

GESTALT PRINCIPLES

Figure and Ground

Individuals perceive the environment as a total unit of meaning, responding to the whole of what is seen. This whole is composed of the stimuli to which persons attend directly, and those to which they do not attend directly. Focused attention organizes environmental parts into a visual whole, a gestalt that emerges as a figure dominating a field of impressions. For example, the margins and spaces between letters on this printed page help to define the words and sentences. If there were no margins and spaces, it would be difficult to distinguish what had been written. Although the white margins are blank spaces, they do not have blank functions. They are integral to the perception of the words. Likewise, all information, whether visual, physical, semantic, emotional, or interpersonal, is gained by relating a figure meaningfully to the field of impressions against which it is perceived.

Gestalt Formation and Completion

Personal experience occurs in terms of figure and ground relationships. The immediate situation in which a person may find himself or herself is constructed from the individual's awareness of self, awareness of the environment, and awareness of the relationship between the two. This awareness of the relationships involved in a particular situation constitutes a gestalt, a meaningful pattern or configuration. Formation of gestalten is conceived of as a natural process, and their formation and completion follow simple principles.

Completed experiences, those that have been successfully resolved in the immediate present, fade into the background of a person's experience as something else comes to the foreground to be dealt with. When clear resolution of any experience occurs, the process of forming and completing gestalten functions very smoothly. Life becomes a series of emerging gestalten and the completion of those gestalten as the individual lives totally aware of the present and functions fully in the present.

In order for gestalt formation and completion to occur naturally, a person has to be able to function in the here-and-now; any experience or reactive pattern of behavior that is held over from the past, or anything that is being anticipated about the future, diminishes the amount of attention and energy persons can apply to the present. Since a person has a limited amount of energy with which to engage the present, the more a person puts energy into concerns about the past and into anticipation about the future, the less that person is able to cope with something here and now. In fact, not only does it mean that less energy can be placed into the here-and-now and less awareness of what that here-and-now actually is, but the present here-and-now experience becomes highly colored by concerns or behavior patterns from the past and anticipation about the future. Under these conditions, the configuration or the pattern that may be experienced by the individual is not the thing as it is, not what is occurring, but some highly distorted interpretation of what is happening.

Emergent Needs

Early work with brain-damaged patients led Kurt Goldstein (1939) to an organismic theory of human personality that stresses the psychobiological whole of each individual. A similar conception of behavior underlies much of the original conception of Gestalt therapy and remains a theme that resounds through all the basic writings (Perls, 1972). Gestalt therapy maintains that each person, as an organism with internal physiological, psychological, and biochemical processes, exists in the context of the total environment. "Internal" processes do not operate in isolation. People depend on organism-environment interactions for nourishment in myriad forms; they also contribute to the regulation of the larger environmental context through their interactions with it. They interrelate with their environment as whole organisms.

What an individual attends to is conceived by Gestalt therapy as related to organismic need and need reduction, as well as the need for wholeness. Needs arise, come to the foreground, and recede progressively as they receive attention and are satisfied. This continuous perceptual process has been expanded by phenomenological psychologists as a model of general human functioning (Combs, Richards, and Richards, 1975). Once fulfilled, a need recedes from prominence and others emerge to be fulfilled; they, in turn, recede from prominence when fulfilled. In perceptual terms, a person's perceptions at any time will center around the clear image; his or her behavior will be directed toward satisfying the dominant need.

The healthy formation of gestalten is a continuous process of emerging figures and receding fields. The highest priority need will emerge from a complex of needs. The satisfaction of needs requires the use of aggression (life force or energy) to encounter that which is nourishing and satisfying in the environment. It requires discrimination to reject that which is toxic. The nourishing part of the environment is assimilated in order to achieve satisfaction. Once satisfied, each need will recede from prominence and another need will emerge, leading to a new gestalt. Awareness will result in the completion of the present gestalt and the emergence of a new one (See Figure 2.1 in chapter 2).

Since a gestalt is irreducible, it will disappear if it is divided into components; a division, as an alteration in perception, creates a new gestalt. The act of perceiving is essential to the creation of figure-ground relationships. Although there is a tendency to conceptualize gestalt formation and completion as a process that occurs with or without the individual's participation, in fact, the individual is not separable from the formation of gestalten. Personal awareness of the figure-ground relationship is integral to the relation. Meaning emerges from the perception of the relationship between the figure and the ground of an individual's unique experience.

Clarity of Gestalten

Clear perception of the immediate present leads to "good gestalten," well-formed or well-represented relationships. Such good gestalten are most likely to occur when individuals have no unfinished experiences that vie for attention and interfere with one's clear perception of the present. To handle present demands well, a person needs to be able to clearly see the necessary relationships among important elements of the current experience without importing concerns from the past or about the future.

Successful functioning may be seen as effective problem solving, whether of a cognitive or an emotional nature. When solving problems, the formation of a clear and meaningful gestalt produces a solution that is often accompanied by immediate recognition of its appropriateness. Confusion is dispelled. There is no mistaking the experience and its structural relation to the context and to the self. Thus it is that we "recognize" clear gestalten; they are right, understandable, encompassing, and we know them.

If there is a problem to be solved, persons may have what Kohler (1973) calls an insight, an "Aha" experience. One might describe that experience by saying, "Something just clicked into place and I knew exactly what to do." The classic example of an "Aha" experience is that of Archimedes who, while he was taking a bath, suddenly realized the principle of displacement of water by a mass. His recognition of the physical principles he had been seeking was so powerful that awareness of other events around him disappeared. As the story goes, he leapt from his bath, dashed into the streets without pausing to dress himself, and cried out, "Eureka!" ("I have found it!"). The gestalt of that one experience was so clear and encompassing that it eradicated other possible gestalten, such as awareness of the social conventions of proper attire in public.

In the natural gestalt formation process, needs, desires, or interests arrange themselves according to principles of clarity and prominence. The primary rule followed is: the most pressing need determines the clearest figure. Gestalt therapy accounts for particularized and even idiosyncratic needs within individuals as a process of gestalt formation and completion based on perceived needs related to perceived aspects of the environment.

Awareness and Attention

In the process of forming a complete gestalt, that of which a person is aware becomes an ordering principle. In fact, one of the contributions of Gestalt therapy has been to focus on the therapeutic validity of awareness, defined as the perceptual flow of figures to figures in a lively progression, as determined by needs. The adequate functioning of awareness dictates the realm of health for the individual. Awareness is lively, characterized by arousal and signaling gestalt formation as well as completion. F. Perls, in fact, claims that awareness itself is curative (1969).

Awareness and attention are important phenomena for the Gestalt

therapist to understand. They are not synonymous. Attention is consciously effortful, but awareness is not. Paying attention signals a pur-
posive focus, made intentional by directing perception toward a particular target. Attention may be spontaneous, an orienting reflex related
to unusual sensations that occur in the environment, such as a fire-
cracker exploding unexpectedly. Attention may also be forcibly directed, in which case it will not be accompanied by the awareness that
always signals gestalt formation. There will be no "Aha!" of recognition.

Although we may not often be aware of choice, we do choose what
will be the controlling figure-ground relationship of situations. For example, if an individual chooses to see a group of people at a cocktail
party as phony or hypocritical, that choice will color whatever is seen
and will order all awareness around characteristics that are congruent
with that choice. If the same individual decides that these same people
are witty, urbane sophisticates, perceptions of their conduct will center
around appropriate conforming details. What might be a sprawling,
haphazard conversation would differentiate into spontaneous sophis-
ticated repartee in one frame of reference or onto a plotted and planned
manipulation of others from another orientation. The mental "set" to
respond to certain environmental cues organizes our perceptions and
our contact with the world. Such a set probably has been learned and
incorporated into a conceptual framework that may militate against a
healthy figure-ground process.

If people apply "brain power" to their experience of the world and
through force of "will" construct a viable reality, they succeed in
thwarting the essential experiential modes of being, and the "will" becomes the organizing focus. Good gestalt formation is accomplished
through spontaneous awareness. It cannot be forced or willed, for it is
composed of whatever awareness and concentration are brought to the
situation plus the excitement produced in merging attention and situation. Any change in awareness merely produces a different total experience, but not necessarily in ways a person "wills."

Closure

An important organizing principle of gestalt learning theory is that
of *closure*. In our perception of the world, we tend to view incomplete,
visually presented information as being complete and meaningful. A
circular line that is not quite connected at each end will be viewed as a
circle; typographically incomplete letters, if they still retain the main
elements, will still be interpreted as meaningful letters; objects with
minor parts missing, such as a television set with the control knobs

missing, are still understood as being the same objects. Gestalt learning theory uses such phenomena as evidence of a tendency to complete perceptually incomplete experiences. Likewise, in Gestalt therapy, there is the recognition that people strive for closure in their personal relationships, even when such closure is difficult to achieve. The tendency to dwell upon incomplete experiences, to return to and relive them, or to carry around unresolved emotions regarding them, prevents the individual from attending fully to figure-ground relationships in the present.

In Gestalt therapy we also understand that in most situations people believe in and strive for finished products or gestalten. We like a sense of completion and fulfillment. It is comforting to point to a physical, tangible object as something we have taken to completion. Early research in Gestalt psychology (Zeigarnik, 1927; Rickers-Ovsiankina, 1928) highlighted the tension created by unresolved, incomplete experiences. Someone may be working on a meaningful activity and reaching a point where the activity is nearing the end but is not completed. Interruption of the activity at that point will lead that person to think about and come back meaningfully to that unfinished activity more frequently than if complete closure had actually been reached. The Zeigarnik effect demonstrates that individuals seek closure; what we really want and what we are looking for in our lives are complete experiences. When they are complete, they are whole, and they can then merge into the ground of life experiences so that another focus can emerge.

Holism

When holistic principles of dynamic change are applied to psychological theory and to therapy, one's focus centers on the whole person. This means recognizing not only the individualistic nature of a person's organizing and experiencing of events, but also that each person is more than an add-sum composite of behaviors, perceptions, or dynamics. Within each person is a movement toward wholeness. Indeed, this recognition is central to Gestalt therapy. A gestalt is, by definition, a whole that is different from the sum of its parts, having the qualities of completeness and meaning. Some therapies and some theories consider only a few elements of the person, disregard the rest, and assume they are making truly meaningful sense out of that person. This is not so in Gestalt therapy.

From the Gestalt therapy orientation, reductionistic approaches that, in conducting therapy, center only upon part of the individual deny too much. They deny the physical in order to have the mental; they deny the internal to look at the external and the obvious to observe the hidden. Holistic approaches affirm the complexity of persons and events; all relevant dimensions are included. F. Perls, early in his writings, revised psychoanalysis in order to remove what he saw as faulty attention to isolated psychological concepts. In *Ego, hunger and aggression* (1947), he proposed an organismic approach that was intended to supplant purely psychological therapeutic approaches with holistic principles. In the years that followed the original publication of that book, he and his fellow therapists succeeded in integrating many aspects of Western psychoanalysis, Western philosophy, and Eastern philosophy into a coherent and far-ranging therapy that attests to its holistic concerns and its wide applicability within and without the therapy setting. Other potent influences were Jung, Reich, and Rank (M. Polster, 1987).

The wholeness of any moment, like the wholeness of a person, is not merely a convenient concept or a psychological point of view. Even though it is important to understand holism intellectually, an intellectual understanding is only a partial one. Gestalt therapy rejects the use of mere logical analysis in therapy and in psychological theory; it has been overplayed in Western culture as the *sine qua non* of knowing and is only one aspect of intelligence. In this rejection of simple intellectual knowing, great emphasis is placed on non-Western intuitive dimensions, drawing upon nonempirical evidence and events. Although it is easy to reject such methods as being nonscientific or nonempirical, we overemphasize the Western analytical bias, unless we are willing to immerse ourselves in the holistic vision that Gestalt therapy embraces.

In *The Field of Zen* (1970), D. T. Suzuki presents the conception of the self as a holistic existence that cannot be divided into parts and separated from the rest of the organism. Suzuki tells the story of the debate between the Buddhist philosopher Nagasena and a Greek king Milinda in which Nagasena, following the scientific method, asked the king to declare what the chariot was in which the king had come to the debate. Was it the wheels, the body, the yokes, or some other part of the mechanism? The king had to answer that the chariot, in fact, was none of these parts. The chariot could not be found in enumerating its parts. The point made by Suzuki is that with pure intellect we can separate the existing elements of things, but in so doing we fail to find what we search for.

ORGANISMIC FUNCTIONING

Intelligence

Organismic self-regulation comes out of direct organismic experiencing. People often suppress awareness of sensory phenomena to such a high degree that they find it difficult to regain awareness of even simple sensory experiences. Of course, some of this is highly desirable adaptation. To endure even an hour in a congested, dirty area of a city, one must be able to mask the noise level, shorten one's breath to keep from coughing or choking, tune out exhaust smells, squint one's eyes to filter particles of soot and smog, and ignore the physical discomforts of jostling crowds and hard pavements. On the other hand, what is lost in this shutting off of the sensory input is an awareness of processes that continue, even when one is unobservant. Since the human body naturally functions as a whole with all its sensory apparatus mobilized or ready for mobilization, movement of the organism into unawareness through "switched-off" modes of sensing severely limits the possible experiences one may encounter.

Organismic knowing is "nonrational" or "intuitive" rather than intellectual "knowing about." Rationality or intellect is only a part of organismic intelligence. This distinctly Eastern way of describing thought rejects "mere" rational thought as striving too hard for control over the environment, including the individual's internal environment, at the expense of simple experiencing. We do not have to "think" in order to feel our muscles move when we move; nor do we have to reason out the colors of trees, sky, and dirt, or compute the sound of thunder. All of these activities and our perceptions of them continue whether or not we think about them. However, we may be so solidly engaged in thinking and talking that sometimes we become convinced that our thinking causes physical phenomena.

Self-Regulation

Self-regulation is a spontaneous, integral, natural part of the organism, biologically as well as psychologically. Spontaneity involves participating in situations in terms of themselves and not in terms of external controls or devices. When the organism regulates itself in harmony with its own nature—and this is not easily done—the individual behaves spontaneously and naturally. There is no effort of planning or doing; there is just being.

Gestalt therapy theory assumes that in every aspect of its "being" the organism strives for organismic balance or creative adjustment (Perls et al., 1951). However, given the holistic approach, changes in external events and new emerging needs create constant change and make it impossible to remain at a balanced point for long. Nor does the organism "want" to remain in a constant, balanced state. In physiological processes, balance is only momentary; as the dominant need of one moment subsides, the next most predominant need emerges. As Walter B. Cannon (1963) points out, homeostatic processes in the organism

maintain biological constancy through complex stabilizing arrangements. It has also been proposed by Piaget (1952) that behavioral rep-
ertories develop through a balancing process, called equilibration, that
regularly incorporates new ways of organizing knowledge or behavior
into the old established cognitive organization. Both approaches to
homeostatic processes underline the fact that life is a constantly fluc-
tuating process, not a matter of reaching completion or termination of
activity.

By trying to make part of a total process into a "thing," we destroy
the process. For a cogent analogy for the homeostatic process, let us
imagine children playing on a seesaw. Two children can arrange themselves in such a way as to be perfectly balanced, i.e., suspended in the
air at both ends, but it is not interesting to them to remain balanced
for very long. For our fantasy children, it is more interesting and involving to move up and down, changing the balance by changing position or by pushing harder or easier.

Psychologically, when we reside at the balance point, we have energy available to go in any direction. We can recognize the potential
for movement in any direction without investing in any of the alternatives or attempting to maintain a still point. F. Perls et al. (1951) call
this "creative precommitment": Note the difference between idling in
"neutral," where no force is applied forward or backward, and strain-
ing forward with the brakes set. The first is a situation of "resting,"
whereas the second is one of extreme conflict. "Creative precommitment" is the indifference-point of a continuum, poised between but
aware of and interested in the potential situations extending in either
direction. One feels the beckonings to action, but is not yet committed
to either side (Perls et al., 1951).

A person can be committed to actions without denying the validity
or the existence of homeostasis within. While doing something, one
may be aware of the freely flowing movement, the adjustments and
shifts made to accommodate oneself to the world. Someone may see
that he or she is engaged in a moment that is part of an unfolding
relationship with the world. Although attending to the foreground experience, the person does not neglect the perspective afforded by the
whole figure-ground relationship. Since balance comes out of active
gestalt formation and completion, attending to foreground experience
in those terms is accepting the process of adjustment and balance. People can maintain psychological homeostasis only by maintaining a holistic orientation toward process and interaction.

In addition to seeing oneself as being in balance with life processes,
the individual may also direct attention to the balance in the world. In
fact perceptions of self and of others are synchronous. Often the as-

pects one assumes about the world are also those one assumes and acts upon within oneself. If one believes in the finitude of the universe, one will also believe oneself to be finite. If the world is seen as a series of objects to be manipulated and controlled, self-manipulation and self-control result. If the world is seen as an objective phenomenon, having intangible, empirical qualities, the individual will be perceived in the same way, as a static film clip rather than as a moving picture. Even though the picture is clear, it is static, not alive and vital. The recovery of vitality and liveliness is a pervasive focus for Gestalt therapy (Polster and Polster, 1973).

Gestalt therapy theory further assumes that all persons who go to therapy have within themselves the energy and resources necessary for self-regulation to function satisfyingly. By saying that each person is whole, Gestalt therapy lays the foundation for assuming that healthy self-regulative patterns and processes are available. Since wholeness is the vibrant, meaningful quality of the successful integration of parts of the individual, the individual's concern is to reach integration. Regardless of clients' statements that may emphasize weakness, dependency, and lack of ability to manage their lives, the therapist must assume there are latent self-regulatory mechanisms of health within each client. The wholeness of persons is not merely a convenient concept or a psychological perspective; it is the bedrock of Gestalt therapy.

The act of personally engaging in a therapeutic relationship is a signal that enough energy can be made available to insure the experiences of wholeness and to empower the self-regulatory processes. Although manifestations of health may be blocked or subverted at the time a person enters therapy, the Gestalt therapist assumes there is a thrust toward personal health that can be strengthened during therapy. This assumption is a powerful component of successful therapeutic engagement with a client.

Polarization and Identification

Polarization is the process through which an individual organizes and symbolizes beliefs about self or about the world. It may either help or hinder self-regulation. In essence, it entails establishing either-or categories or niches into which one classifies events or perceptions. Often, these classifications are made according to evaluative criteria, such as good-bad, interesting-boring, worthwhile-worthless, acceptable-unacceptable. Such classifications may polarize emotions (love-hate, sincere-insincere, etc.) perceived attributes about the self (me-not me, good child-bad child, etc.), or perceived attributes of others (friend-enemy, helping-hindering, significant-insignificant, etc.). Such designations establish constructs that often become rigid, uncompromising, and unchanging (Kelly, 1963).

Polarization occurs when an individual identifies strongly with one end of a set of opposite characteristics. In Gestalt therapy, it is understood that the polarization process leads frequently to misattributed self and self/other definitions and a tendency to invest more and more energy in maintaining the pole with which a person has identified. A further result of such polarization is the subsequent denial of experiences or characteristics that do not conform to the person's existing constructs.

It is recognized in Gestalt therapy that polarization of feelings, attitudes, or values enables the individual to establish definitive bases for relating to the world; it provides a simple structure for experience by reducing the complex, relativistic phenomena a person encounters daily to discrete, predictable elements. The individual then finds it easy to interpret events and to determine appropriate responses to those events. Such structures may be experienced as safe; they may also be constricting and stultifying.

During the course of a person's life, however, more and more experience may be reduced to dichotomous constructs, which means that more and more experience becomes predictable and, through that predictability, the individual loses a sense of aliveness. Over a long period, the individual may become inured to feeling half alive and experience that condition as being an acceptable adjustment to the world.

The Gestalt therapist believes the primary motive for rigid polarizations in the individual is to combat fear by establishing control over various aspects of the environment or of the self. By mentally pigeonholing experience, the individual uses a two-value reference system to create labels or constructs regarding life, and then proceeds to respond to the adopted labels as if they were, in fact, the same as the event they categorize. Control derives from the power of such labels, giving a false perspective of the range of the experience. This may mean, in the long run, that people develop expectations that all things fit into neat categories. When they don't fit, extreme discomfort arises from the dissociation of the individual from the safety of established categories. The Gestalt perspective affirms the validity of both ends of the polarization and the appropriateness of either in certain cases or situations. Both love and hate are valid emotions; both good child and bad child constructs may exist in the self-structure of the personality.

Differentiation and Integration

The process of identifying is a process of denying; a person denies one end of the polarities in order to identify with the other end. At the time a person may seek to restore a balance, it is common for him or her to experience an impasse, a blockage of energy and attention that prevents effective solutions to problems occurring in his or her life. This impasse needs to be explored in such a way as to reveal the hidden conflicts within the person and to facilitate resolution.

To accept denied parts of the self is not an easy process for many people because the impetus for denial that led to the original rejection or disowning can remain within the person. It may still be threatening to accept characteristics that challenge long-standing beliefs about oneself. The therapeutic processes that lead to acknowledgement of the truth restores the self-regulating process where healthy emergence of needs and awareness occurs spontaneously. Early in life people may start learning ways to halt that self-regulation by denying parts of themselves. As F. Perls says, we in effect cut off pieces of ourselves and say that anger is not me, that hate is not me. The individual has to identify with those disowned parts; they can not be affirmed and integrated until they have been acknowledged.

As a self-organizing, self-regulating organism, the individual finds a balance by restoring the parts that had been denied for so long. The restoration of balance returns the individual to homeostasis; he or she then functions spontaneously and responds to events as they occur, making appropriate choices based on immediate awareness.

ILL HEALTH (NEUROSIS)

Thus far we have primarily discussed principles of healthy functioning, along with a few allusions to ways in which health may be disturbed. In Gestalt therapy, neurotic ill health consists of particular disturbances—disruptions of the self-regulating processes of gestalt formation and completion. Such disruptions are survival-oriented, powered by fear of becoming lost or hurt or fear of losing love or attention. In the absence of love and supportive attention, survival dictates that the self be manipulated by tensing the body, censoring natural processes, burying pain deeply within, and cutting off awareness of present experiences. Survival also dictates that the environment be manipulated for support. In manipulation, no risks are encountered and no contact with disturbing experiences is made.

Neurosis is signaled by "confusion, boredom, compulsions, fixations, anxiety, amnesias, stagnation, and self-consciousness" (Perls et al., 1951, ix). All of these are manifestations of the self or of the environment and are discussed at length in chapter 3.

Principles of Therapy

At times, Gestalt therapy has been described as being concerned only with "I and thou, here and now" relationships. Although such characterizations are simplifications of essential Gestalt processes, those twin concerns are central aspects of the therapeutic system. "I and thou" refers to contact, an essential ingredient of therapy; "here and now" refers to the change process that occurs via contact. Five other key concepts in Gestalt therapy are change processes: *affirmation, clarity, appropriateness, respect,* and *experimentation.* Each of these aspects of the Gestalt system will be discussed thoroughly in chapters 4 and 5; the theoretical principles associated with each concept will be outlined at this time.

Contact. Contact has been identified as "spontaneous concentration" on something, as "the sense of the unitary interfunctioning of you and your environment" (Perls et al., 1951). In Gestalt therapy, the contacts that are important are both intrapersonal (contact between the client and aspects of himself or herself) and interpersonal (contact between the client and perceived aspects of interactions with individuals or events from the past, present or future). Since contact includes a sense of the interfunctioning between client and environment, spontaneous concentration on any aspect of the environment carries with it the energy for movement or change. Contact between the therapist and the client has been called an "I-Thou" relationship (F. Perls, 1969), taking the label and the sense of the power of the relationship from Martin Buber.

Buber (1958) describes casual contact between people as an I-It association. Aggression beyond the contact-boundary has been achieved for contact; however, the quality of the contact is business-like or habitual, not incorporating significant contact, which is denoted as an I-Thou relationship. When two or more persons are completely present, completely real and aware of each other in their interactions, the I-Thou relationship flourishes. Gestalt therapists use the I-Thou construct because the therapeutic encounter necessitates the presence of the client and the therapist. That is, both the client and the therapist must be attentive to what is happening in the here-and-now of the therapeutic environment. An I-Thou contact, then, facilitates change.

Change Processes. Contact generates the necessary energy for change to occur. The important change processes are not connected with trying to change. Gestalt therapy is a process-oriented therapy. The therapist does not limit the targeted phenomena to the problems, confusions, conflicts, anxieties, and depressions that the client relates. The client's perceived problems and expressed reasons for seeking therapy are not discounted, but the focus in therapy may go beyond the stated concerns. Interventions, appropriately timed and directed, may lead the client to an experience and an understanding of the forces and resistances within the client's experience. The intervention, thus, may delineate more specifically what is being experienced and also may expose when the problem emerged and how the problem is being maintained. Change happens through present-centered, spontaneous concentration on any figural aspect of the client's experience, including the client's experience of the therapist's responses. During such concentration, the client may acknowledge a personal truth and affirm its validity in the client's life.

Affirmation. An ingredient of the contact experience that promotes change is affirmation or acknowledgment. Recognition and affirmation of personal truth in present experiences brings a cessation of conflict or confusion because completion of an important gestalt occurs at that time. When a personal truth is denied, ignored, or repressed, the individual's investment of energy in confusion or conflict is extended, and the fear that powers the investment is fed. Affirmation is simply saying "Yes", the key to conclusion of the therapeutic work. The content of the affirmation at that point is immaterial with respect to completing the gestalt. While the client may not approve of the experience being affirmed, affirming it—saying, "Yes, that's true!"—is essential.

Clarity. The experience that results from acknowledgment or affirmation is clarity. The goal of Gestalt therapy is not to encourage a particular kind of personal experience nor to bring about a particular kind of choice. The goal is to bring clarity out of the confusion and conflict the client has been experiencing. The client's clarity after a gestalt has been completed enables decisions and choices appropriate to his or her experience.

Appropriateness. There are no prescriptions for the kinds of life decisions a client should make. When the primary goal is clarity, the client's decisions reside within her or his own purview. A therapist may respond when asked for an opinion but only if the therapist judges the opinion will not be introjected (swallowed whole). It should be chewed, deliberated upon, so that the client can make a personally responsible choice. The concept of *appropriate* also describes the kinds of interventions or responses the therapist makes in the therapeutic context. Clients differ in the problems they report in therapy in their internal and external resources. The Gestalt therapist has interventional strategies available that are limited only by creativity and clinical judgment exercised through contact with the client. These strategies are oriented toward exploring underlying dynamics and processes and can be used appropriately when the therapist is well aware of the client's resources for change.

Respect. In contacts with the client, the therapist demonstrates respect for every aspect of the client's systems—the healthy, self-regulatory mechanisms and the mechanisms that block healthy functioning. The authority in the life of the client is the client, not the therapist. Although therapists may have intense personal or professional reactions to what clients relate, the demand Gestalt therapy makes on therapists is that they respect, in every way, the client's experiences. Although respect does not connote approval, it does mean that the therapist becomes a participant-observer in the therapeutic encounter, paradoxically being present and contactful but simultaneously reserving personal judgment in favor of neutral observations. Sometimes, as primarily participant, the therapist shows respect by challenging the client's statements or actions. Sometimes, as primarily observer, the therapist provides necessary and appropriate support. In the process of therapy, the client is the arbiter of appropriateness, since it is the client's life experiences and observations that provide the raw material for therapy. The client's limitations are respected even when they are not accepted as reflecting the limits of growth in therapy; the client's clear decisions concerning any aspect of his or her life are respected.

Experimentation. In the safe emergency of the therapeutic relationship, the client is encouraged to experiment with experiences that may generate awareness or remove blockages to self-regulation. Usually, interventions are organized around here-and-now experiences, although the methods are as varied as the number of Gestalt therapists. The successful conclusion of such an exploration of process leads to empowerment of the client and to the release of aliveness and vitality—"the Gestalt outlook is the original, undistorted, natural approach to life" (Perls et al., 1951, p. viii).

PHILOSOPHICAL ASSUMPTIONS

Underlying the psychological theory of Gestalt therapy are ontological, epistemological, and axiological issues (Van De Riet, Korb, and Gorrell, 1980). We shall now examine in abbreviated fashion these philosophical issues as they correspond with the Gestalt perspective.

Everything that exists is a process having as its main features change, flow, mobility, happening, and relation to other things. Every thing that exists is also a part of a whole, a oneness, a totality. Knowledge itself is of two kinds: descriptive or intuitive, depending on whether the knowledge is of parts or of a whole. Knowledge itself, whether it is knowledge about an entity or simply awareness or attention to that entity, is a gestalt, an irreducible phenomenon that cannot be analyzed or explained without altering the phenomenon and creating a new one. Thus, to know is to observe and be consciously aware of experiences in the present. The organism "knows" through its total intelligence and, in responding, it exhibits its process of "knowing."

Viewed as an integrated individual consciousness, instead of a passive register of data provided by the external world, each person constructs a personal and unique world of sensory awareness of the environment and of the structures, images, meanings, and knowledge ascribed to awareness. From these constructs, the person chooses personal interactions with the world, attitudes, feelings, and actions. The person also symbolizes these attitudes, feelings, and actions in words, bodily movements, images, and dreams. Both individual and environment are affirmed in the Gestalt perspective, and the involved consciousness of the individual becomes the active creator of the personal experience of the world and the communicator with the world in the interaction process.

To place awareness, symbolization, and choice at the center of the Gestalt model is to make a phenomenologically oriented appraisal of how life is lived, how gestalten are formed, dissolved, and reformed. And underlying this orientation, as we just noted, is an affirmation of the individual and of environmental processes as they exist, not as they are said to exist or as one might wish they had existed. Both of the latter—the beliefs about and wishes for the individual and the world —are phenomena to be dealt with. What is, is; what we do, we do. Existence, then, is whole and authentic. No aspect of living is to be avoided. All is affirmed. All may enter awareness or be the focus of attention. All individuals choose from their experiences what they will and as they will.

Finally, in this process of creating and experiencing one's world, no legal or moral set of ethics and values can be superimposed on personal experience without doing violence to the one who is experiencing. One may make a choice to live in situations accepting such a set of superimposed values; one chooses, in such a case, to violate personally held standards or values for the sake of something or someone with a higher priority or a stronger demand. The valid ethical stance in Gestalt therapy is based on the situation in which the interaction takes place. All persons are responsible for themselves in that interaction, and for the choices made in the existential moment.

SUMMARY

The essence of Gestalt therapy is an understanding of organismic gestalt formation and completion within each person's experience. Events are experienced in figure and ground terms, a natural process of emerging figures that have meaning in terms of the context or background against which they are experienced. This process is an integral part of spontaneous self-regulation. Needs of the individual emerge spontaneously through homeostatic process and are resolved as other needs emerge. Gestalt therapy assumes that (1) every organism is creatively adjusting to the self and the environment at all times, and (2) such creative adjustment is possible because each person who enters therapy has the energy and resources necessary for self-regulation. Neurosis results when natural self-regulating mechanisms are disrupted.

Principles of therapy—contact, change processes, affirmation, clarity, appropriateness, respect, and experimentation—derive from the basic gestalt principles. Philosophically, Gestalt therapy falls within the existential, phenomenological, and creative/ethical orientations.

Chapter 2
Psychodynamics

In Gestalt terms, the whole of Gestalt therapy is the ground, the background or context for this book. In each chapter, we concentrate on one aspect of Gestalt therapy which then is the figure that emerges from the field. Thus far, we have considered as figure the psychological processes, therapeutic principles, and philosophical assumptions. Now, in chapter 2 we look at psychodynamics—personality structure and personality dynamics—as figure before moving on to definitions of good and ill health (chapter 3), change processes and the course of therapy (chapter 4), therapeutic interventions (chapter 5), and the person of the therapist (chapter 6). First, we will look at personality structure from the Gestalt therapeutic perspective and then expand the discussion to personality dynamics.

PERSONALITY STRUCTURE

Each person experiences perceptions, needs, wants, thoughts, interests, and emotions fluidly through a process of gestalt formation and completion. Figure-ground relationships that emerge for the individual in experience are satisfied or resolved spontaneously, or are put aside unfinished; they then recede from prominence in the individual's flow of experiencing, and other matters emerge into awareness. As figures recede from prominence, some are retained in the ground of experience as relatively constant constructs, beliefs or attitudes. The process of developing figure-ground relationships, however, occurs within the organism continuously in dynamic, on-going formations. Personality, then, in the Gestalt therapy approach, is essentially structured out of the figural interactions within the individual and the interaction between the individual and the environment, as a set of basic structures and a process of on-going changes. Out of the flow of experiencing, basic personality structures have coalesced in the ground of experi-

ence. These structures may be seen as a relatively constant set of constructs, attitudes, and beliefs about the individual and the environment
which exist as part of the person's ground.

To fit Gestalt therapy into the theoretical psychological field of personality dynamics, we may say that it is related to Goldstein's (1939)
organismic theory, and to the phenomenology of Lewin (1951), Rogers
(1951), and Combs and Snygg (1959). Boulding's (1956) formulation of
the imaging process provides a key component as well. The structur-
alism of contemporary French psychoanalysis (Lacan, 1956; Mucchielli,
1970), which incorporates the individual's symbol systems (particularly
language) as primary factors in the individual's structuring experience,
is also related. In their early work, Bandler and Grinder (1975) also
discuss the language systems of the individual in a manner that is congruent with the Gestalt therapeutic approach.

Healthy functioning of the individual involves appropriate, dynamic
interrelationships among the individual's experiencing of self, of others, and of the world. The dynamic properties of the individual are the
most important; experience is ever-changing, on-going, constantly in
process. However, to understand the relationship involved in this dynamic structure, we need to look at conceptions of organism and self
from the Gestalt therapy viewpoint.

Organism

The organism is a totality of the essential aspects, parts, or organs
functioning as a complete unit in persons. The organism, then, is the
term or concept used to denote the total unit of any given person,
including biological and psychological structures, functions, and processes. To set the stage for later discussions of therapy practice, we
now proceed to an elaboration upon the practicalities of gestalt formation and completion as they are lived out in the lives of clients.

The organism operates according to gestalt formation and completion principles; its primary functions are to be aware of and to regulate
internal needs, and to interact—in Perls' terms, "to aggress"—with
the environment to meet those needs. Out of the total phenomenal
experience, the organism attends to the most compelling, urgent, interesting, or potentially satisfying aspect. Whatever an individual se-
lects will be a product of the interaction between perceived needs (not
necessarily overt and, certainly, not necessarily conscious) and perception of the offerings of the situation (Combs and Snygg, 1959). Gestalt
therapy affirms an internal valuing process that functions on a survival
level and on a level of elaboration and satisfaction of basic needs.

On the basic biological level of organismic responses, simple needs
for such things as food, water, and shelter occur. On more complex

levels, even though the process is the same, it becomes more difficult to specify in advance the particular needs of the organism. The problematic aspect of that which is experienced by the individual is not necessarily identified consciously; an organismic reaction that orients the individual toward pressing needs is the more important identifier. Gestalt therapy is so insistent upon the capacity of the organism to function without conscious decision-making, given certain necessary environmental conditions, that many therapists and theorists have identified consciousness as the creator of problems and solutions to a person's discomfort and unhappiness (F. Perls et al., 1951).

With this idea, we return to a consideration of the importance of closure of unfinished situations, for there is a powerful need within the organism to gain completeness and a sense of wholeness—gestalt closure or completion—in its activities. In moving toward wholeness, the organism encounters past experiences within itself that have not been resolved which cry out for resolution. These incomplete gestalten surface in the same way that biological needs surface, one at a time. The most pressing one becomes the most clear. When functioning without interference, then, the organism is self-regulating. Each need emerges from the field of experience; the individual discriminates and takes action ("aggresses into the environment") in order to satisfy the need; when the need is satisfied, the gestalt is completed and fades into the background; the next need then emerges.

Since each gestalt is individualized and emerges from the inner need system, the material required for closure also is individualized; the sense of closure is uniquely that of the experiencing individual. This closure brings a sense of peacefulness, completeness, and rightness that can be understood only by the experiencing organism in its totality. At the point of closure, the body experiences the wholeness and the mind stills or rests as tension, associated with unresolved conflict, ceases. A gestalt, then, is an aesthetically experienced whole, not a rational or cognitive whole which can be communicated directly to another. Gendlin (1967) denotes this experience as the exact moment when the words or symbols accurately express the person's inner experience. At that moment, nothing else needs to be expressed.

The Gestalt therapist believes that the organism is motivated and activated by the search for wholeness, and in that search the organism is self-regulating and will meet all of its needs if it is interacting with an ideal environment. Each gestalt formation-conclusion cycle would lead to satisfaction and no unfinished business would remain. However, we do have unfinished business. Each of us has been born with certain hereditary tendencies that may be limiting; accidents may have inflicted physical, psychological or spiritual limits; and we have developed psychological styles, patterns, and coping mechanisms that are rarely ideal for our needs as we have interacted with an environment that often is not ideal.

Let us look more in detail at the process by which the organism attempts to satisfy its needs. First we shall state the process as it is self-regulated and then examine blockages and limitations to that process.

Figure 2.1 presents a graphic representation of the gestalt formation-completion cycle. We have chosen to present this cycle in eight stages. Each stage is an important psychological process in meeting a need.

Stage 1 represents the organism at rest. The background of experience is undifferentiated, filled with all of our unfinished business along with all of our life's gestalten plus our need in the form of wants, interests, thoughts, emotions, etc., all quiescent. In Stage 2, arousal occurs as one need emerges or becomes figure. This could be any physical, psychological or spiritual need, or it could be a signal from an incomplete gestalt from the past. Although there are an untold number of wants, desires, interests and pieces of unfinished business in the background of experience, the organism can deal effectively with only one at any given moment. Some Gestalt therapists add the element of need clarification at this point. For example, if hunger is aroused, clarification would involve becoming specific about what kind of food a person wanted or needed.

During Stage 3 the organism scans the environment and/or itself to see what possibilities, options or choices are available to meet the need. Continuing with the example of hunger, we might see the kitchen in our mind's eye with an open refrigerator or we might think of three restaurants or two fast-food outlets. Stage 4 involves choosing one of those options—a certain restaurant perhaps—as the best way available to meet the need.

Stage 5 is contact or action. Here we must do something, make some change internally or aggress into the environment. In the example of hunger, we would go to the restaurant and do what was necessary to obtain the food to eat. Stage 6 is assimilation or rejection. Here, the organism receives, takes in, or absorbs the new material—the change, feeling, or physical nourishment—or the organism rejects the new material as inappropriate, unnourishing, or unnecessary. Stage 7 involves experiencing the satisfaction of the assimilation or appropriate rejection, thereby reducing the need. In Stage 8 we let go of all that has happened from Stages 2 through 7 so that the gestalt process can begin again with the next arousal. This may mean ordering a different kind of food or going to a different restaurant.

Let us follow the cycle through another example. Suppose a man comes home from a difficult day at work. He is vaguely aware of discomfort as he enters his home. Actually, he is hungry, tired, has sore feet, is carrying concerns from the office, and feels a lack of nurturance

Gestalt Experience Cycle

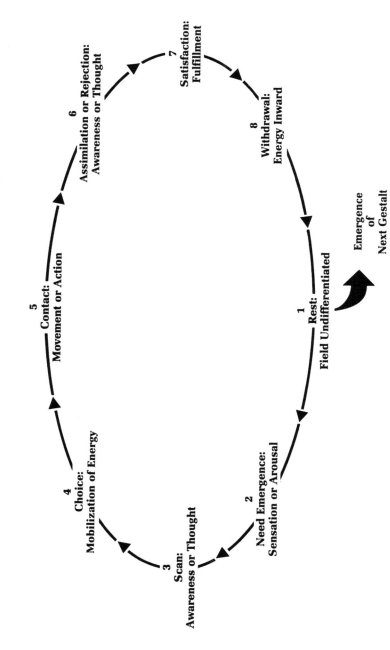

FIGURE 2.1. Gestalt Experience Cycle. This illustrates the stages in beginning and completing a Gestalt. The stages are explained fully on page 24.

25

from others. However, these needs are undifferentiated. As he enters, the need for nurturance emerges as the dominant need. He clarifies the need by becoming aware that he wants a nice loving hug from someone who cares about him. He scans his memory and knows that he can get such a hug from either of his daughters or from his wife. He sees that his daughters are involved with a friend and notices his wife sitting in the living room. He decides to go to his wife. He walks into the living room, puts his arms out, and says, "I need a hug." He pulls his wife up from her chair, embraces her, and she responds lovingly. He takes in the nurturance, enjoys it, and feels the satisfaction. He then relaxes for a moment and becomes aware of his sore feet. A new gestalt cycle has begun related to sore feet. This basic gestalt formation-completion process repeats itself in myriad ways each day of our lives.

In the above examples the cycles are completed; however, if we interrupt, block, obstruct, interfere with, or impede this cycle, or if the environment does not present the needed result (the man's wife is not available, for example) we are left with partially or totally unmet needs and we experience unfinished business. One way the organism has of attempting to assimilate and resolve important unfinished situations is to bring them up over and over again. For example, you may have some unresolved conflict with your brother who wears a full beard. At a party, you are introduced to a young man whose beard resembles your brother's. The sight of the beard may trigger thoughts and feelings about brother that prevent you from either seeing the new young man clearly or listening to him attentively. This is an ineffective way of dealing with either the new or the old experiences. It may create more unfinished business in the lack of contact with the new person. When past experiences remain unresolved, they impinge upon the present; they obscure clear need formation, obstruct responsiveness, restrict movement, and limit activity; they prevent closure for which the organism is internally motivated. Enough unfinished and unclear situations can produce a neurotic individual who employs great amounts of energy and many kinds of debilitating processes in avoidance of contact with self and with others.

Cognitive controls placed upon the organism deny its intrinsic ability to regulate itself, in addition to keeping the organism in a constantly incomplete and unfinished state. By placing inappropriate controls over the emergence and expression that leads to organismic balance, the individual undermines this important assimilation process. While self-regulation is a natural and spontaneous activity in the organism, internalized methods of control, adopted through attempts to "adjust," may interfere with this activity.

Taught from childhood that natural impulses, natural movements, and needs are dangerous, many persons learn to keep them caged or on leashes, like ferocious beasts. However, such controls are not necessarily beneficial; instead of allowing persons to move toward completion and wholeness, they often delay and deny the assimilation process. Control of this type counteracts genuine, authentic expressions of needs. The excuse or reason persons control themselves is either a moral one ("shoulds" or "oughts") or a defensive one, a fantasy concerning what might happen without careful control. Catastrophic expectations concerning consequences for spontaneous behavior inhibit the individual's free expression and open responses to situations. For whatever reasons they are instituted, such controls lead individuals to distrust the natural, organismic needs within and to doubt their ability to satisfy those needs.

A simple example of such control may help to clarify this point. You are sitting in a committee meeting with members of a planning group who are actively engaged in a productive discussion. You have missed your lunch. You, however, do not interrupt the meeting either to declare your hunger or to go get something to eat. You stay in the meeting and control your attention so that hunger takes second place to the content of the discussion, although it interrupts your attention regularly. While your control in such a situation is often functional in the immediate context, habitual or characteristic control may lead to ignoring, repressing, or distorting the cognitive and motoric processes that keep the organism functioning as a complete system.

Gestalt therapy refers to early and continuous interference with self-regulatory mechanisms as leading to neurotic functioning or neurotic styles (Shapiro, 1965), such as obsessive-compulsive, manic-depressive, narcissistic, paranoid, hysterical, and passive-aggressive processes. A child in a family system that is based on "shoulds" and "oughts" learns that system very early in life, even if that set of prescriptions is never verbalized. The child introjects (absorbs wholly without reflection) the system: it then becomes a set of ideations about right and wrong, including ideations about being a good or bad person based on adherence or lack of adherence to the system of prescriptions.

When the child breaks the rules, the child learns that he or she is a rule- or lawbreaker and internalizes that sense of self. The child develops constructs that say, "I am powerless to get what I really want," "I am a victim," "I am the wrong one," or "I am not OK." The dynamic of punishing the self for perceived transgressions may become a controlling system that successfully interferes with the self-regulating processes within the individual. Interruption of a self-regulated system requires external manipulation in order to continue the functions that have been blocked; one has to take conscious control or make habitual deliberate decisions for otherwise free-flowing activities or awareness.

One of the tasks of the Gestalt therapist is to use all of this background material with each client to ascertain where and how clients interrupt the gestalt formation-completion cycle and intervene to encourage awareness of the interruption. Referring to Figure 2.1 (page 25), interruptions may occur at each stage. At stage 2, clients may not indentify needs clearly, or they may experience needs as overwhelming and give up at this point. Clients may vaguely be aware of two or three competing needs and not allow any one to become dominant. At stage 3, scanning may be done too fast or superficially, or in too much detail. Options may be discounted; some good options may be unknown. At the choice point (stage 4) some clients see their various choices clearly but are unable to select one; others are clear as to what they want to do to meet their needs but block at stage 5, afraid to take any action. At stages 6 and 7, the cycle may be disrupted by an inability to assimilate, receive, or reject the consequences of the contact; therefore, the individual may block the experience of satisfaction. Blockage at any of these stages sends unfinished material into the ground of experience and prevents the next cycle from emerging.

Most individuals develop patterns that interrupt the gestalt formation-completion cycle. These patterns eventually become habitual, leading the individual to experience that discomfort of incompleteness as a normal part of life. It is such patterns of blockage that Gestalt therapists are most interested in working through with clients.

Self and Self-Concept

Self-As-Process. The self-as-process has been articulated cogently by F. Perls et al. (1951). We paraphrase their seminal discussion in the following paragraphs.

As the organism responds to its own needs and regulates its responses in order to meet or satisfy its needs, it makes contact with the environment. F. Perls (1947) calls this "aggression" into the environment. Through these contacts or aggressions, the distinctions between the organism and the environment are sharpened. Awareness of these contact points is one aspect of the "self." In fact, F. Perls et al. (1951) claim that the self actually is the organism's system of contacts with the environment, and, as such a system, it integrates all levels of needs. In addition, it evaluates what is appropriate for the organism, the knowing of what is true for the organism at any moment.

One way to see how the self operates is to reflect upon a time of

particularly intense needs and activity, possibly great stress or heightened emotions. In such a time, persons experience contact with surroundings in sharply defined terms and experience the evaluation of
what is appropriate or true with clarity and immediacy. Let us consider
an example at this point. You are driving down the street thinking
about the shopping list you have decided to take care of when a car
starts up from the side of the street and moves out in front of you.
Immediately, the contact with that stimulus supersedes the thoughts
you have been attending to, and total awareness of the environment is
sharp and clear. Your "self" has organized your perceptions around
the immediate need to see the situation clearly. Then comes the evaluation, in this case almost spontaneously. The need to stop short of
hitting the other car leads you to jam on your brakes and swerve. That
need arises from the "self's" evaluation of the event, choosing self-
preservation, knowing what to do to best accomplish that, and activat-
ing the foot on the brake. These are not conscious, thoughtful decisions; they are the "self" in action. In many known cases, the organism responds in such immediate crisis situations with feats that seem
almost superhuman. The usual conscious decision-making processes
are not involved at all. The total organismic power is available without
contamination.

The evaluation process enables the person to monitor actions and
statements according to how "true" they are. When engaged in various
routine and nonroutine activities, one may violate an inner sense of
what is "right." When this occurs, evaluation of one's behavior follows
and through nonverbal reactions informs the individual of the truth.
These activities of the self are internal, sometimes derived from momentary awareness and sometimes carried out in an unaware state until a conclusion is reached. In either case, one aspect of the self is the
system of awareness to contact with the boundary between self and
not-self and to the evaluation of the awareness and the self's responses
to the contact.

The feeling of "rightness" in one's expressions and experiences has
been indicated by many psychologists as an important identity experience. Erikson (1968) describes a process in which the individual is more
vital and animated in daily functioning as being one in which the person overcomes some estrangement and is able to react holistically to
the environment; that is, at some deep level the person "solves" a
"problem" or resolves an identity dilemma. Earl Kelly (1962) says that
the fully functioning personality knows no way to live except in keeping with personal values, which means that in the basic experience of
oneself, in the exploring and discovering of meaning, the person has a
subjective experience of valuing and of being in touch with the totality

of individual identity. Horney (1945) explains that the loss of spontaneity, the power to experience oneself freely, leads to alienation and emotional sickness. Maslow (1954, 1962) suggests that one can choose wisely
from one's life only if one is capable of listening carefully to one's needs
and wishes. Rollo May (1969) suggests that through repression of experience modern individuals have lost their images of themselves as
responsible individuals. F. Perls (1969) echoes this statement when he
divides the word responsibility into response-ability, suggesting the
central importance of each person's ability to respond in individual
personal experiences.

Self-As-Concept. A second aspect of the self is the self-concept or self-
image. This aspect of human functioning was not clearly recognized
nor elucidated in the earlier edition of this book. A growing recognition
of the functions of belief within the individual has led to the incorporation of self-concept into the description of human processes. Gestalt
therapists in on-going practice have confronted the realities of clients'
symbolizing their experiences in particular ways and have perforce been
acknowledging the importance of the self-concept in therapeutic efforts
with clients.

Among the most prominent self-concept theorists, the self-concept
is portrayed as a collection of beliefs about oneself, arranged in a hierarchical structure (Combs and Snygg, 1959; Coopersmith, 1967; Marsh
and Shavelson, 1985; Rosenberg, 1979; Stryker, 1979) and having direct
influence on one's behavior. It has long been recognized that there is
not a unitary self-concept, but a collection of concepts ranging from the
relatively enduring and influential to the relatively trivial and evanes-
cent concepts of self. The conditions under which self-concepts change
have been variously described as being based on evaluations from culture and family (Rogers, 1951), influential feedback and encouragement
from significant others (Combs and Snygg, 1959; Coopersmith and
Feldman, 1974), comparison with others (Wagner, 1983), and success
experiences (Purkey, 1970). Of special influence, however, is the individual's assessment of feedback and experiences in terms of self; Combs
et al. (1976), for example, following a phenomenological model of self-
concept, posit that change in the self-concept occurs only following
some new experience of self. Objective reality notwithstanding, unless
the individual perceives feedback and successful experiences as being
successful, there will be no change in self-concept. Since individuals
construct their own beliefs about themselves, they are the ultimate
sources of self-concept change.

During the individual's lifetime, concepts or images that enable the
person to interact with the environment (Boulding, 1956) coalesce into

a self-concept. If, as mentioned earlier, I have learned from childhood that my natural impulses, movements, or needs are unacceptable and must be subjected to strict control, I may develop a belief that I am unnatural and unacceptable, unless I am completely under control. I will then monitor or interrupt my set of contacts with the environment. If I have learned from childhood that I can do no wrong, a concept of myself may be that I am deserving of obedience from everyone. If all of the messages about myself absorbed from childhood seem to say only that I have great potential, I may conceive of myself as being unable to develop that potential because I never have developed it.

These kinds of images of the self may be embedded in nonconscious aspects of the person, and may be valued and perceived as essential for psychological survival. These values are relatively static and resistant to change, because they are considered by the individual to be true.

Process and Concept Interaction. Self-as-process orientations emphasize the on-going, organismic interactions of the individual with the environment as it is; self-as-concept orientations emphasize the structure of the individual's beliefs about self and about the world. These distinctions are complementary, not antithetical. A person's contact boundary contains the active processes of attending, perceiving, evaluating, and choosing based on the interactive contact point. Decisions about behavior, which may violate a person's self-concept, however, may redefine the interactive points and lead to changes in responses. The self-concept is thereby a touchstone for monitoring the appropriateness of decisions made at the point of contact with the environment.

For example, in a therapy session, a client has been describing an encounter with his major professor in his doctoral program. In the conversation with his professor, the client did not say what he really felt and what he really wanted to do about his dissertation research. As he describes the situation in the therapeutic setting, the therapist and he interact at the point of contact between them; the client describes the encounter with his professor and then begins a process of checking on and choosing responses freely. The therapist suggests that he say aloud, in the confines of the therapy session, what he really would like to have said. The client's body stiffens, his breathing becomes shallow, and he looks away from the therapist. His self is experiencing fear and is reminding him that actually he is powerless and cannot acknowledge his real thoughts and feelings even in the safe environment of the office. The concept of himself as powerless has limited the kinds of interactions he allows himself to make.

Both self-as-process and self-concept may be targeted in Gestalt therapy. Self-as-process may be observed by the therapist in both the client's verbal and nonverbal behavior. Self-concept, however, has been developed through years of one's interactions with the world; it, too, may be changed by therapeutic interactions, but the change typically is slow. The self, as a totality, is a multifaceted set of beliefs and processes that include awareness, knowing, and choice. At times, the individual may be conscious of the self-system and its processes; at other times, the self may operate and the individual not be conscious of the processes. Chapters 4 and 5 concentrate on the therapeutic structures and interventions appropriate for work with self-as-process and self-as-concept.

PERSONALITY DYNAMICS: THE PROCESS OF EXPERIENCING

In considering the basic structure of personality, it is inevitable that we consider also the dynamics through which the structure operates and changes. This consideration derives from the shift in emphasis, in the past ten years, from primal intrapersonal issues to both intra- and interpersonal issues. As will be seen in the later sections on practice, this shift has been fueled by a shift in emphasis from Perlsian workshop therapy to on-going re-creative therapy. We now can take a closer look at how the personality functions as a whole.

Contact and the I-Boundary

In the self-in-environment equation there are three items: self, environment, and the interaction between the two. The interaction with environment in Gestalt therapy is called *contact*, and the points of contact constitute the contact boundary. By definition, the contact boundary is the locus of points at which "one experiences the 'me' in relation to that which is 'not me' " (Polster and Polster, 1973). The experience of the contact at a person's environmental boundary involves both an experience of self, an experience of "other," and a skill in discriminating the relationship between them. The paradox of the contact is that it differentiates and relates at the same time; it is "felt both as contact and as isolation" (Perls, 1947). The contact boundary is not fixed for all time; for all persons, it is a dynamic relationship, changing moment to moment as they experience themselves as well as aspects of the environment that become figural. Change is the nature of the contact boundary.

Contact may also occur with aspects of oneself. Since humans have the ability to become self-observing, they may experience parts of themselves as part of the internal environment by clearly differentiating those separable parts into meaningful units. Such self-contact may be growthful or disruptive, just as contact with the external environment may be growthful or disruptive.

Contact happens between two clearly delineated, clearly discriminated entities, leading to a response characterized by attraction or repulsion. Contact, however, is limited by an aspect of the person known as the I-boundary (Polster and Polster, 1973). Each person has limits as to the kind and quality of contact that is permissible. As the Polsters note:

> The I-boundary is composed of a whole range of contact boundaries and defines those actions, ideas, people, values, settings, images, memories and so on in which he is willing and comparatively free to engage fully with both the world outside himself and the reverberations within himself that this engagement may awaken. It includes also the sense of what risks he is willing to take, whether opportunities for personal enhancement are great but where the consequences may bring on new personal requirements which he may or may not be up to (1973, p. 108).

Within the I-boundary, contact is easy; at the I-boundary, contact is more risky; outside the I-boundary, contact is difficult.

The kinds of choices made at the boundary determine the life-style, the nature of the chosen community, the work experience, the home, family, or love relationships that are permitted or avoided. The rigidity or permeability of the I-boundary determines the quality of interactions with the environment. Since each person is multifaceted, each person has body-boundaries, value-boundaries, expressive-boundaries, and exposure-boundaries.

In Gestalt therapy theory, contact or clear choice at the I-boundary is recognized as healthy. Almost always, when clients come for therapy, however, their contact functions are not healthy in certain ways. The therapist is one facet of the client's environment, and in the dialogic relationship between therapist and client the unhealthy, contact functions become evident. In the presence of anxiety or depression, the body-boundaries, familiarity-boundaries, expressive-boundaries, or exposure-boundaries may be too constricted, too rigidified, or too permeable. In the presence of confusion, the value-boundaries may have become uncertain or indistinct. One of the goals of Gestalt therapy is to sharpen or educate the client's awareness in order to guide the client to a recovery of healthy contact functions.

Zones of Experience

Earlier, we identified three structures in the personality according to Gestalt therapy. Now let us consider three zones of experience: interior, exterior, and intermediate, or meta-experience. The processes that occur in each zone and the interrelation among the zones determine the individual's levels of functioning and personality development.

The interior zone, which includes the organism's experiences of itself, is defined as the experience of everything that occurs within the body. This zone includes mood, emotion, proprioceptive stimuli, hunger, thirst, adrenalin surges, and so on. It does not include awareness of the quality of the experience or the process of it. While a knowledge of physiology, biology, or neurology may aid in an intellectual understanding of the range of interior experience, the individual's own experiential awareness of body states is the focus for our discussion at this point.

The external zone incorporates experience of the immediate external environment gained through the senses. Awareness of the external world is processed through the individual's eyes, ears, nose, throat, and skin, and personal associations with the phenomena being experienced, not through purely "objective" characteristics. Thus, the quality of peppermint candy is realized as sweetness, or texture, or a certain flavor, not as a chemical formula or a physical mass. The experience of sweetness becomes mingled with the interior experience of the body and, in fact, may become a part (usually short-lived) of the interior experience, as when a slight taste of peppermint remains in the mouth after the candy is eaten. At this point, we experience the taste as part of ourselves.

The prior simplified example indicates a necessary, though often subtle, process of interrelation between exterior and interior experiences. Is this interrelation simply one of changing an exterior experience into an interior experience by receiving it in the personal framework? Not necessarily. Some exterior experiences, that is, experiences of the external environment, affect the internal processes only so long as the external phenomenon exists. An example would be the experience of the hardness of a bench. Other experiences of the environment begin a process of assimilation that continues as an internal experience for varying amounts of time after the phenomenon itself has gone, such as an event that calls forth a complex of associated emotions.

The point of transfer from exterior to interior experience, the intermediate zone, varies in many ways, most of which depend on the attitude of the person involved. An obvious example is chewing and swallowing food. At some point—and this is likely to vary considerably with individuals—the commingling of food and saliva turns this external substance into part of the person. Some persons may recognize this food as part of themselves, even before they swallow it; others only recognize it when it is assimilated through the digestive system, an internal process activated by, but not part of the external phenomenon of food. Elimination of waste products continues this process to the final separation of the waste product from the body.

F. Perls (1969) calls the psychological contact between external and internal contours the DMZ, the demilitarized or middle zone of experience. Triggered by both the interior and exterior zonal experiences, it is in the service of neither. The DMZ may be realized as memory, fantasy, imagery, dreams, wishes, labels, etc. In short, it is meta-experience—experience about experience—that mediates, improves, destroys, biases, organizes, but profoundly influences the quality of the interior and exterior zonal experiences. The capacity, in individuals, for meta-experience entails the separation of cognitive functions from other experiential functions.

If you do not understand clearly the difference among the three zones, the following experiential exercise may help. As you read the following paragraph and allow yourself to follow the simple directions, you may experience each of the zones and begin to differentiate the zonal experiences.

> Stop. Pay attention to what you are hearing for a few moments. . . . The sounds you hear put you in touch with the external world. They give you sense impressions. . . . Now notice any feelings you have in your stomach. . . . This puts you into contact with your internal world of experience. . . . Now think back to what you heard when you were listening. Did you put a label on it? Did you categorize the sounds in any way? If you heard a sound and thought, "That's a bird singing," or "That's a car engine," you were in your DMZ or middle zone of experience.

In the above exercise, if you allowed yourself to follow the suggested series of experiences, the only contact you had with the external phenomena (i.e., bird singing or car engine) was the sound waves hitting your eardrum. You did not see the bird, feel it, or touch it, yet you figured out that it was the bird singing; or a car engine making noise, or an air conditioner humming. What you added to the sense experience came from cognition, the middle zone. Similarly, if you felt tension or fullness in your stomach and gave it a label, a meaning, or an interpretation (i.e., "I'm feeling excited" or "I'm feeling full"), you were adding a middle-zone experience to the experience of the body state.

All interpretations, labels, qualifications, images, and so forth are associated with the middle zone. Any contact through the senses with something outside the individual is experience of the outer zone, and any feelings that come from inside the individual are experiences of the inner zone. Often, we become confused by believing that how we process or think about an exterior or interior experience—our image of the experience, for example—is necessarily a part of that interior or exterior experience itself. It is not. The exterior or interior experience is an immediate and spontaneous sensation or contact. Middle-zone experience is not a sensation, not contact, not immediate or spontaneous. Lack of clarity in one's discrimination between these zones leads to confusion between experiences of fantasy and reality, which is discussed later in this chapter.

Gestalt therapy is not unique in recognizing the ways in which the individual misinterprets reality by attaching inappropriate labels to experience. Rational-emotive therapy (Ellis, 1958) also concentrates on the process through which an individual misconstrues events. According to Ellis, when people experience an event, they interpret it according to their own belief systems. Irrational beliefs about the world generate emotions within each person, but persons tend to believe that the event they experience "causes" their emotions, instead of recognizing they are their own source of emotional reactions. For Ellis, therapy attempts to change a person's irrational beliefs to rational ones, for it is through such changes that a person becomes capable of developing more realistic concepts of the world and of the self. What Ellis calls "irrational beliefs," F. Perls refers to as fantasy. Although therapeutic interventions are very different in the two systems, both Gestalt therapy and rational-emotive therapy emphasize the importance of accurate, realistic perception as a prerequisite for healthy functioning.

Symbolization

Each person has, as the most characteristic endowment, the ability to symbolize all aspects of personal experience (Boulding, 1956; Cassirer, 1953; Langer, 1951). In understanding even very simple phenomena, the individual draws upon the capacity for symbolizing in diverse ways. An event may be symbolized in order to be communicated to another person, in order to be remembered by the individual, or in order to be explored mentally more fully. Mental activity in itself, whether it is engaged in abstruse theoretics or in the everyday manipulation of objects, represents phenomena. Not only does it mediate experience, it re-presents it to each person.

In the symbolizing process, mental activity transforms undifferentiated impressions into recognizable patterns, such as figure-ground arrangements, which are related by individuals to the whole of their synthesized experiences. Thus, symbolization is the essence of mental life, giving the individual the ability to go beyond mere absorption of incoming impressions. The ability to symbolize allows the individual to remember past experiences, anticipate future events, establish interchanges in the present, and determine the personal meaning of them all.

In terms of personality, symbolic functions enable the individual to experience existence in a self-reflective manner. That is, on one hand, individuals are immersed in private perceptions and their views of and beliefs about the world are controlled by those perceptions. If private perceptions were the only means of responding to the environment, the individual would not be able to reflect upon actions, but would merely be reacting automatically in the way the autonomic nervous system reacts to stimuli. On the other hand, a person is capable of construing experience in a variety of ways and thus is controlled more by constructions of reality than by objective events.

Self-perception is possible because symbolization is possible. Symbolization of experience begins as a simple tool for sorting out the impressions and events that impinge upon a person, labeling of experience for example. It becomes an elaborate process of understanding, eventually extending beyond the labeling of immediate phenomena to describing phenomena not immediately accessible to the senses. The self and the perceptual process are both displaced from immediate experience; because they can be symbolized, they become accessible to each person.

What we are suggesting is that only because the individual is capable of both perceiving and abstracting from perceptions is he or she able to develop processes for changing experiences and altering self-concepts. Symbolization processes, then, are primary processes in therapeutic interventions—language, imagery, dreams, abstractions of body experience.

The ability to abstract and symbolize reality and to symbolize oneself in appropriate fashion are complementary processes. With the ability to abstract, the individual increases the ability to function adequately. However, the capacity to abstract appropriately is not a function of intellectual prowess but of perceptual style. Concentrating on overintellectualization or categorizing experience tends to divorce the individual from the world as a whole. For example, in a study of the experiential abilities of reluctant witnesses to crimes, Denner (1970) found that persons who are most hesitant about informing store owners of observed shoplifting tended to maintain a conservative, rigid orientation toward their own experiences as well as toward external experiences. Denner found that an overintellectualized orientation toward symbolizing concrete experience leads to a conservative state in which the individual maintains a rigid overcontrol regarding the interpretation of events. His subjects exhibited a similar overcontrol in problem-solving situations and when asked to describe themselves in open-ended, contrary-to-fact situations.

In the healthy personality, organismic experiences are brought to conscious awareness through appropriate symbolization. Symbols enable the individual to make contact with the deepest levels of experience; their status as experiential signals leads to the organization of images and meanings within the individual. It is through signals that the most complete experience of oneself as an independent entity emerges.

The subjective feeling of having a self and of having experiential processes that arise from within oneself are important ingredients in the healthy personality. Without the ability to hear inner signals regarding needs and to respond directly to them, the individual lacks a sense of "rightness" or congruence in the whole of experience.

A case concerning the importance of symbolizing personal experience comes from the private practice of one of the authors. George, the client, was described in the following way:

> He had no sense of being a real person; he felt himself to be an empty shell that functioned, but with mist and vapor inside and no solidity or strength. I perceived George to be personable, above average in intelligence, and to have an excellent command of the language. In fact, George talked a lot—about himself, about his family, about his animals, about his schooling, about his job prospects, about his girlfriends (or lack of), about his apartment, about his car troubles, and on, and on . . . and on. He talked a lot. After several sessions, George confessed that he felt totally unconnected from his voice and his words, which came as off a tape recorder and floated away in space (Korb, 1974, p. 12).

George's divorce from the words he spoke highlighted the experience he had of not being in touch with himself as an experiencing, meaningful person. He had no valued personal symbols or images, no labeled body-sensation experiences to give a sense of stability to himself.

On the level of self-perception, the practice of categorizing, according to good or bad, leads to denial of some aspects of self and overidentification with other aspects. The symbolization of personal experience through dichotomous labels and constructs interferes with open awareness of one's own potential. Such limiting constructs are products of the DMZ or middle zone of experience—the intellect that is exercising overcontrol of the flow of human experiencing.

Contact-Withdrawal

If boundaries do not meet, they cannot interrelate. If they do not interrelate, there is no contact. The means of contact with the external environment are the senses: seeing, hearing, touching, tasting, smelling, and concentrating attention on sensory information. The senses are the organs at the boundary between self and not-self, giving information that enables the person to distinguish and discriminate in ways essential for healthy functioning.

There is no growth without significant contact. A plant will not grow without establishing contact with the soil for minerals and water; and the air for oxygen, carbon dioxide, heat, and energy. There is no mistaking the soil for air or the minerals for the plant itself. Contact comes out of the necessary distinction between the plant and the soil. Thus, also in humans, contact occurs only when there is distinction; otherwise, the various aspects of person and environment would be one object—the same object. Without distinction, there is only oneness and, hence, no opportunity to make contact, to vary, to assimilate otherness, and to grow. The lack of clear definition and difference is called "confluence" in Gestalt therapy. It will be discussed in the chapter on good and ill health.

The polar opposite of environmental contact is withdrawal—not loss of good contact, but transference of good contact from the environment to internal processes. The rhythm of one's perceptual processes includes a constant flow of contact and awareness among the three zones. That is, contact through the senses with aspects of the environment— seeing the color of the sky, hearing the sounds of trucks or a police siren, touching the rough bark of a tree or the hand of a friend, tasting the sweet-sour essence of catsup, seeing the words on the page as you read—and then withdrawal into the inner zones to awareness of a knot in your stomach, a warm glow in your chest, or a tense, tight area in the back of your neck . . . and then on to awareness in the middle zone (DMZ) with thoughts, memories, reflections, fantasies, planning processes, goal-setting strategies, or rational step-by-step problem-solving mechanisms.

We have stressed contact with the environment in the early discussion. However, similar clear and distinct withdrawals into the other zones are also essential for optimum functioning. Withdrawal from contact must also include the physical retreat from a challenging and stimulating environment to a restful environment. This withdrawal-awareness of experiences inside the skin may be of such things as opposing points of view, mixed emotions, conflicting desires or attitudes, tight or tense muscles, painful responses in any part of the body, or bodily actions or movements. By differentiating the separate elements in such inner experiences, a person may become aware of healthy or unhealthy aspects of personal identity. In Gestalt therapy, participants are encouraged to become more aware of themselves in ways that will clarify the diffuse, perhaps confused, parts of themselves. With clear awareness comes the completion of gestalten; healthy and growthful experience is then possible.

Identification-Alienation

Because of the associations a person may have regarding any particular object or person with which contact is made, the individual tends to establish either identification with the person or object, or alienation from it. Generally speaking, it may be possible for someone to identify strongly with all aspects of the world and, thus, to accept and appreciate whatever enters experience. However, this condition of acceptance, according to Maslow (1954), is a rarity, occurring only during "peak experiences" in a person's life. For most persons, the more common and pervasive experience is one of partial identification with and partial alienation from various persons, experiences, or characteristics of oneself. Thus, the identification and alienation processes are characteristic of the individual and determine many of the variations in personality between persons or in one person from one time to another. Each of us identifies to varying degrees with what we are, what we think we are, what we want to be, and what we think we need to be. In identifying, we polarize experiences into good and bad, I and not-I, beneficial and detrimental. Our sense of self solidifies, at least momentarily. By differentiating between the acceptable and unacceptable within ourselves, we cast our lot with the portions that most support our own view of ourselves.

We accept from others, or experience in others the things we cannot mobilize or identify within ourselves. If we do not affirm ourselves— truly find ourselves satisfactory—then we are inclined to expect others to provide the missing aspects. In a similar fashion, we tend to expect the external world to provide us with what we do not provide ourselves. These expectations may not be a part of our consciousness of ourselves. However, the self, as it identifies with or alienates itself from aspects of the environment, is functioning consciously, attending or not attending to input from outside as it chooses. Identification with particular events, objects, or persons arises out of seeking need-fulfillment through them.

The identification-alienation process may lead to unhealthy responses to the environment, depending on the individual's identification object, the object related to positively. If one identifies with unreasonable demands, one is alienated from the real self and from healthy contact. One may then begin to expect from the environment opportunities to maintain the identification. When one's expectations are not fulfilled, when one's demands are not met, a person develops resentments. Since most people are taught that their resentments are improper, unexpressable, or impolite, they are likely to suppress them. Holding back on the expression of resentment, however, makes it difficult to communicate with others. An important effect of unexpressed resentment may be the feeling of guilt people attach to it. They feel guilty about the built-up resentments, and then do to themselves—in Gestalt therapy this is called retroflection—what they really want to do to someone else. They make demands on themselves. This neurotic guilt leads to a "should" or a "should not." "I should like him." "I should not be resentful." "I should not expect her to meet my needs." They punish themselves in this way and make themselves feel guilty instead of expressing their resentment.

Guilt itself is experienced as identification with a demand that people be better than, or at least different from, what they are and that they control their feelings and their thoughts. However, since people cannot live up to all of their self-expectations, nor to all of the expectations others have of them, resentments of failure are common. In every experience of guilt, there is a nucleus of resentment—a hanging on to the status quo, neither giving up the investment in the situation or person nor ventilating the anger. It is easier to identify with the guilt feelings—particularly since virtually everyone has some feelings of guilt to draw on—than it is to identify with resentment toward someone else. Therefore, guilt becomes an acceptable, even a normal alternative to the recognition of underlying resentment.

Behind most neurotic guilt and resentment lie demands directed toward others. These demands may also be so threatening to self-esteem they may not be confronted directly. Failure to confront and express demands, then, leads to the build-up of resentment toward others for not living up to the often unexpressed expectations, or for not anticipating those expectations. Behind such resentment toward others and alienation from them, lies alienation from unacceptable characteristics within the self. Thus, there are emotional blocks based on identification with some aspects of the self—loving, caring, or performing well, for example—and alienation from others—resentment, hostility, anger. In therapy, a person may be able to own the feelings of resentment, thus reducing the guilt, and then clarify the demands and expectations that led to the resentment. The process of immediate contact with each emotional level opens the possibility of healthy identification and eventual acceptance of personal responsibility.

Some guilts are not neurotic; they reflect a reality of actions that might have been more effective or appropriate to certain situations. A person may intrude into another's life space (i.e., ignore the contact boundary) and experience guilt subsequently. Such guilt is more accurately stated by the individual as an awareness of responsibility. Rather than making an internal statement such as, "I am *guilty* for not returning your telephone call," the individual can say, "I am *responsible* for not returning your telephone call." In cases like this, the individual really has created an interpersonal problem, but is able to resolve it effectively by properly accepting responsibility for it instead of labeling it in neurotic fashion.

Re-owning personal responsibility through identification with personal expectations makes it possible for clear demands or assertions to be made and clear responses given. If you say, "I demand that you do this for me," you are responsible for yourself; you have owned your own demands. Then the person being addressed can respond to the demand by saying whether or not he or she is willing to fulfill the demand. Both persons will know what is being said and what is being responded. Each is responsible for personal behaviors. When agreement is reached, both persons experience closure—gestalt completion. If there is disagreement, both will know where the differences lie, and these may be worked out in a guilt-free way or may be accepted as they exist. Either way, gestalt completion occurs.

Besides expressing resentments and demands in order to seek solutions to conflicts, their expression often leads to appreciations of both the self and the other person. There is almost always some residual benefit in whatever situation people find themselves, but they are sometimes so immersed in the negative aspects they are not free to pay attention to what may be appreciated. For example, Frankl (1963) gave birth to logotherapy and its attendant philosophy in the concentration camps, in Germany and in Poland, in World War II. For Frankl, while this experience was destructive and demeaning almost beyond belief, it gave him what he needed to develop his ideas and to increase his own self-appreciation. This position does not deny negative aspects of any situation; it merely recognizes the ability of the human organism to find beneficial aspects of almost anything, an experience that indicates the validity of the polarization hypothesis.

To review the process we have been discussing, the Gestalt therapy perspective assumes that closure demands direct confrontation with and, eventually, acceptance of feelings of guilt, thus opening the route to recognition and acceptance of demands leading to the acceptance of experiences that may have originally seemed absolutely unacceptable. Closure becomes a matter of how much of one's experience one identifies with and how much one alienates from oneself.

SUMMARY

In this chapter we have discussed individual psychodynamics in two ways. First, we have looked at the structural aspects of personality: the organism as a whole, the self, and the zones of awareness as they are construed in Gestalt therapy. Next, we have dealt with personality dynamics; that is, with a description of the ways in which the structures of the personality operate and change, bringing good or ill health. The major dynamic processes we looked at are contact and symbolization. Contact-withdrawal and identification-alienation are two essential examples of polarized processes. In the next chapter, we deal more particularly with definitions of good and ill health from the Gestalt perspective.

Chapter 3
Good and Ill Health

From the Gestalt perspective, the process of organismic self-regulation is characterized by an innate and unsuppressable need for wholeness, for aliveness, or for the completion of gestalten. As Tobin (1985) has pointed out, self-regulation in Perls' writings seemed to be viewed as an internal psychological or biological process of homeostasis. In the theory and practice of Gestalt therapy today the self-regulation process is seen to have both internal and external components; the person functions within the environment. Self-regulation, while organismic, arises out of both internal processes and environmental interactions. The dialogic nature of human existence is honored. Healthy self-regulation includes a concern for the surrounding communities and environments. Therefore, anything that facilitates gestalt formation and completion and promotes good contact with the environment can be considered healthy. In contrast, anything that blocks, impedes, avoids, or interrupts these processes is unhealthy. Signals of such disruptions may be anxiety and/or depression; forms of such signals may be social, physical, emotional, cognitive, or spiritual. Gestalt therapists consider that any such manifestations may be the target in therapy.

Disease, in the generally accepted view, is illness for which one goes to a doctor who is expected to diagnose and prescribe remedies for cure or relief. The nature of the illness may never be understood; the doctor is the expert who can cure; the doctor controls the situation and is responsible for the patient. In the Gestalt view, ill health is discomfort one may not fully understand, but for which one has some responsibility. Remember that each human being is a self that is continuously interactive with the environment. Each person completes gestalten by reaching for or receiving from the environment the nutrients, either psychological or physical, needed for satisfaction. In reality, each person lives in an environment that does not always offer the experiences that nurture or satisfy organismic needs, or that facilitate the completion of gestalten. Each person, then, has some responsibility for his or herself within the environment, for the quality of the environment (Tobin, 1985), and for the quality and content of the self-environment interaction.

F. Perls notes that societies or cultures may encourage what Gestaltists label as ill health. What societies deem as acceptable ways of being and acting are seen as conforming to societal demands and values for the preservation of mores and social structures rather than validating personal values and the valuing process. Personal validation may endorse some values that are socially acceptable, and also may endorse some that are not.

In an unsupportive environment, each person experiences a dynamic interaction between good and ill health. Each has some combination of the psychological qualities of insecurity, fear, self-doubt, anxiety, inertia, and thoughts and feelings of inferiority, loneliness, hopelessness, powerlessness, and self-pity. Each person experiences some kinds of physical instabilities at times—gastritis, colds, backaches, headaches, as well as virulent kinds of illness. Each person also has another set of qualities associated with psychological health: love, strength, confidence, courage, joy, hope, enthusiasm, trust, faith, and serenity. Each person experiences times of good physical health when all parts of the physical body seem to be fully functioning.

In the Gestalt view, each person is a whole person, and health and illness are experienced psychologically, spiritually, and physiologically with interactions between those systems. Various polarities are present in each person, creating either a balanced or unbalanced functional framework for behavior. In this chapter, we look more closely at the framework of values considered healthy in Gestalt therapy, and at the ways in which health is both encouraged and prevented by both the person and the environment.

GOOD HEALTH

Values

In the course of human development, each person is taught a system of social and cultural values, primarily by experiences with parents and with school environments. Such values might be conformity or complaisance, hard work, making money, having good homes and living in a "nice" neighborhood, revering the mother in the family and family membership itself, being an American or a black or British, or not being an American or a black or British. Many of these values, without the person's being aware, are internalized. Some of these values are consonant with the person's inner self and inner experience, and some are not. To actualize one's own aliveness, one's own inner set of values, inner wisdom, power, love, and potential—to develop one's own inner support system—is one of the central goals in what Gestalt therapists consider as health. All other aspects of health are considered under this general statement.

Some specific views are inherent in the Gestalt view of health. As people mature, they may develop the following qualities of living, all of which are considered to be healthy. Naranjo (1970) describes his list as a set of injunctions regarding desirable ways of experiencing. Therapeutic activities are based upon these values.

1. Live in the "now."
2. Live in the "here," in the immediate situation.
3. Accept yourselves as you are.
4. See your environment and interact with it as it is, not as you wish it to be.
5. Be honest with yourselves.
6. Express yourselves in terms of what you want, think, feel, rather than manipulate self and others through rationalizations, expectations, judgments, and distortions.
7. Experience fully the complete range of emotions, the unpleasant as well as pleasant.
8. Accept no external demands that go contrary to your best knowledge of yourself.
9. Be willing to experiment, to encounter new situations.
10. Be open to change and growth.

Although Naranjo's list was written in 1970, it has not been surpassed as a statement of principles of health. The only additions since then would incorporate truths that might be stated thus:

11. Keep the memories of the past and concerns about the future in perspective.
12. Be available to an open dialogue with the persons, ideas, things, and institutions in which your life is lived.
13. Use the word *appropriate* as a touchstone for your choices.

The experience that underlies this set of injunctions is aliveness, "radiance" (Hycner, 1987), or "inspiration" (Jourard, 1964).

Such principles as those listed by Naranjo are not unique to Gestalt therapy. Many world philosophies would include precepts such as these. It should also be noted that many cultures include value orientations that are opposite; such as, valuation of past and future rather than present or of an outside supreme authority above inner personal responsibility. It is also important to point out that this list is not a list of "shoulds" to work toward. Rather, it is a list of values associated with life and health.

The psychological processes associated with health have two components: intrapersonal and interpersonal. Intrapersonal health is defined as internal clarity—good contact with the intellectual, emotional, spiritual, and physical aspects of the person or, at least, recognition of blocks in any of these aspects. Interpersonal health is defined as appropriate contact with aspects of the environment. Since each person interacts with a unique set of environmental phenomena containing various important values, good and healthy contact may differ from person to person. Healthy contact is the one that is appropriate to each individual's experience.

Now let us consider some of the general positive values in Gestalt therapy. The ones we have selected are maturation, responsibility, self-actualization, authenticity, and contactfulness.

Maturation

Maturation in Gestalt therapy is considered to be an organic process. For example, when a fruit is mature, it is ripe; it contains within itself the essential materials and processes to change its own physical structure and grow as a fruit-bearing tree. A ripe peach falls to the ground; it loses its attachment to the tree, and, in contrast to its previous state, it is self-contained. However, a peach seed in a vacuum will not become a tree. It still needs nourishment, much of which is within the skin of the peach. A proper environment is necessary. After the pulp of the peach is consumed, the peach pit must find further nourishment, this time directly from the earth, air, sun, and water.

F. Perls (1969) defines maturation as transcendence from environmental support to self-support. The peach transcends early dependence upon environmental support, becomes a parent tree itself, and continues its growth. Human maturation proceeds similarly. The first environmental support given up is the safety and warmth of the womb at birth, then the mother's breast, then the need to have people bring food, and so on. Early stages of physical development are successive progressions of transcended environmental support. Likewise, psychological maturation necessitates surrendering dependencies upon outside support in progressive stages of transcendence (see chapter 6).

Since persons are social beings, the process of maturation never results in complete self-sufficiency, but it does move in the direction of self-support in the sense of responsibility for the self and for its support, including asking for help when necessary. We learn to "walk on our own two feet" physically and then emotionally and psychologically, discovering that, as we let go of an external support and take that support function upon ourselves, we develop a sense of self-worth and a more effective use of our inner wisdom and our capabilities for observing, learning, and understanding. Such self-support functions also include the recognition of times when outside help or support is necessary, and the capability and willingness to request that support in nonmanipulative, direct ways.

Maturation is not easy; often, it is accompanied by psychological distress. Each step in the process depends upon leaving the safety and security of a familiar state, even though it may be uncomfortable, and risking the tender self in unfamiliar terrain—moving through an impasse, in Gestalt terms. The old and familiar defenses are no longer functional; there is tenderness and tentativeness in the movements into what is perceived as new and, perhaps, frightening. The old and familiar supports are no longer present. Parents are left at home when a son or daughter goes to school. The school environmental supports are no longer present when a son or daughter takes a job. The old job surroundings are gone when one takes a new job. The parental situation at home, or the school situation, or the job situation may have had uncomfortable elements, even extremely difficult ones; however, these situations were familiar and, therefore, provided some measure of security.

Each step in the maturation process (see chapter 6) involves the possibility of experiencing and developing more of what is possible for each person. Each step stirs fear because the new contains risks. The individual's confrontation with positive and negative potential outcomes creates an impasse as the limit of what seems safe and known is reached. In the Gestalt view, each person has what is needed to risk growth, to develop, and to mature. These capacities are present but unexplored and even unknown. Each move into new experiences draws forth some new aspects of the person. Thus, each move is a self-actualizing experience—the actualizing of aspects of the person not experienced previously.

Each step in the maturation process also involves an increasing awareness of the possibilities of trusting oneself to be able to handle life as it comes. A retrospective look at even very difficult life passages may include the affirmation, "I made it!" accompanied by a sense of self-worth and of trust related to how much has been learned. When the steps are experienced as too long or the new experience is too discrepant or disjointed from the old, the person may experience acute depression, attacks of anxiety, or may begin to behave ineffectively. The maturing person will ask for help at those times.

Along with the development of a sense of self-worth and the awareness of being able to trust the self comes a change in the identification of one's self as the person matures. In the early stages of development, the sense of identity is derived from the responses one gets from important and significant persons who, in some ways, serve as a mirror in which one sees oneself and from which one constructs an identity. This identity may be ill formed or far removed from what one might really be when the authentic self is allowed to emerge and is given the nourishment it needs to grow. Maturation involves a progressive emergence of the inner self, the development of an authentic identity.

One other comment needs to be made. Maturation continues lifelong, as self-actualizing continues lifelong, carrying the potential for change, for growth, for new experiences that add new knowledge and awareness. Experiences plumbed to the depths yield new possibilities for the development of self-support, and trust in the wisdom of the self.

Maturation, then, is a set of experiential steps that embraces other important Gestalt therapy concepts, such as these from our 1980 edition: *responsibility* for personal feelings, experiences, and behaviors and for the choice of appropriate responses to the environment; *self-actualization*, a term that denotes the process of developing more completely what is already present potentially; and *authenticity*, wherein behaviors reflect thoughts and feelings true to the self. Today, in 1988, in keeping with the dialogic approach, *contactfulness* is added. We now turn to a discussion of these concepts.

Responsibility

Being responsible for oneself means being "able to respond" to one's own expectations, desires, fantasies, and actions, and to those of others. It also means shedding responsibility (knowing one is not "able to respond") for the behaviors, attitudes, and feelings of others and for their expectations; but this restriction of responsibility in no way implies a lack of caring about the needs of other people nor does it imply an inability to respond to their needs. When people are responsible for themselves, they know that no one else can respond to the world for them. This kind of responsibility derives from self-acceptance, acceptance of the environment as it is, and from the maturity to see both self and others in proper perspective.

Responsibility, awareness, freedom, and choicefulness are different aspects of the same process. In order to be responsible, we must be aware; to the degree that we are aware and responsible, we are also free to choose our responses, including our actions, thoughts, and attitudes. We are, however, not able to be free and to choose our responses if we are either unaware or consciously do not take responsibility for ourselves.

F. Perls (1969) has stated that taking responsibility for oneself is both healthy and appropriate, as opposed to unreflectively feeling obliged to do for another what one assumes is needed or desired. F. Perls points out that the ordinary sense of the word *responsibility* contains the idea that an individual accepts obligations from others and, therefore, attempts to fulfil those obligations or expectations. Attempting to live up to others' expectations, implicitly or explicitly, entails denial of one's own needs in favor of others' needs. Ultimately, this denial leads the individual away from awareness of his or her own pressing needs and processes.

Each person is responsible for thoughts, feelings, attitudes, wishes, and needs—for self-destructive as well as survival-oriented or self-enhancing desires. Since awareness of personal experience is essential for organismic growth, any experience for which one refuses to take responsibility is denied attention, care, or nurturance. Just like any other growing organism, each part of the individual needs attention and affirmation. Without interference, the parts of the individual that need the most attention will emerge as clear figures against the ground of the person's total experience. Ideally, each person is able to respond to psychological or physiological needs immediately and fully.

The description of responsibility is simple, but the process of being responsible is more difficult. Many people blame others for their problems rather than assume responsibility for their contributions to the problem. Children find it easy to say, "He started it," "It was her fault," or "He hit me first." This pattern is difficult to change. In later life similar responses may be voiced: "The test wasn't fair," "If only my husband were different," or "The real problem is my boss, the neighbors, the children, the government. . . ." Even though the boss or the government may be creating problems for us, the Gestalt perspective focuses attention on the aspects of any situation that the individual creates or chooses to be involved in.

An implication of taking responsibility for one's own behavior and feelings is that each person is also free to choose responses in any circumstance. Gestalt therapy emphasizes this freedom of the individual, and therapists may seek ways of demonstrating to the client the personal freedom that always exists. Without a belief in such personal freedom, the individual typically becomes convinced that there is no way to change. With the awareness that each individual sets limits upon public and private behavior, chooses what is done, decides whose influence is important and whose opinions are valid, comes the awareness of the ways in which each individual sets limits and relinquishes personal freedom.

When someone or something outside of us is allowed to make choices critical to us, we give up or avoid our responsibility in a situation, and we also give up what may be essential freedom. We allow ourselves to be victimized. To realize our own involvement in the process around us is difficult, but it frees us so that we know our freedom of choice, no matter what its target, belongs to us, if we want to take it. Recognizing and accepting this freedom is one of the healthy processes of growth for each person.

Self-Actualization

According to Maslow (1954), the term self-actualization was first coined by Kurt Goldstein in the late 1930s. His studies and observations of the ways in which brain-damaged subjects maintained and enhanced their organismic functioning led to his postulation that the search for ways to maintain and enhance the self is never ending. To the Gestalt therapist, self-actualization becomes possible when people fully identify with themselves as growing, changing organisms. Recognition of oneself as being what one is and not what one wishes to be seems to free one from fantasies regarding perfectibility and the attendant striving for unrealistic and counter-organismic goals.

A paradox regarding the striving for perfection is that the development and pursuit of unattainable expectations actually has a limiting effect upon the individual. By identifying with fantasies that relate to conditions or qualities that should be or might be, the individual ends in what F. Perls (1972) calls "self-image actualization" rather than "self-actualization." Likewise, in persons, such distortion of the self in an effort to become something other than what one is has serious detrimental psychological consequences. The easiest example may be the effort to take the concept of self-actualization as a program for self-development. Although the self-development effort may resound with positive possibilities, psychologically one is denying oneself, an unhealthy state at best. Self-actualization, then, is an organismic process involving the gradual development of one's unique potential through the acknowledgment of what one is.

Authenticity

Authenticity is an important aspect of maturation (Bugental, 1965; Maslow, 1962; Rogers, 1951). More than mere honesty or directness of expression, authenticity refers to the habitual congruent presentation of oneself. That is, the authentic individual is open to the content (thoughts, feelings, etc.) of inner experience and is able to continuously address the world in a manner that validly represents that inner experience. "Congruence" is a term used to designate a moment of total awareness of the quality of the inner experience, the sense of identity with it, and the overt manifestation that exactly symbolizes it —a moment in which a gestalt is completed. Authenticity, as we use the term, refers to the mature state in which such congruence is habitual.

Let us make a distinction here. Rogers and others sometimes speak of being open to one's inner experience as "following one's feelings" and are thought to support an antinomian, antisocial, anti-intellectual view: anything one "feels" is right and good; there is no need to control impulses or to consider the needs and feelings of others. Such a reading of Rogers neglects other aspects of both his theory and practice. Such a reading is often made of the writings of Gestalt therapists, also neglecting other aspects of theory and practice. Gendlin points out that Rogers assumes "the 'feeling' one optimally 'follows' is in awareness and implicitly contains social, moral, and intellectual meanings" (1962, p.255). By "feeling," then, Rogers means any attitudes, beliefs, values, emotions, or cognitions that are truly felt, truly experienced. The Gestalt therapist concurs.

The distinction we make is that such "feelings" in the authentic person are self-validated and are the result of a process of self-awareness and choice. Some "feelings" will coincide with societal values; some "feelings" will deviate from them; and some "feelings" will be idiosyncratic. The authentic self validates experiences of both the self and the environment.

Authenticity is more a by-product of the maturation process than a conscious goal. The person who is free of unfinished business from the past, free of unrealistic expectations of the future, in touch with present organismic processes, and in good contact with the environment will express the self authentically. No other presentation is possible. Even the choice to present oneself in limited fashion for social reasons will be authentic.

Contactfulness

The Gestalt therapy view of the self is twofold: It is seen as both concept and process. We have detailed aspects of the healthy self as concept. The healthy self-as-process must be grounded in contact (Hycner, 1985; F. Perls et al., 1951; Polster and Polster, 1973). In fact, the self in this case may be defined as the system of contacts between the individual and the environment. A person's ideas, beliefs, values, memories, and perceptions interact with awareness of the self at the I-boundary. When the individual is fully functioning, the gestalt formation and completion process proceeds without interruption. Closure will not ensue unless the person makes the appropriate contact with either internal processes or the environment.

Consider the following scene: You are working at your desk and begin to feel hungry. You begin a gestalt about hunger, feel the pangs, and think "I am hungry." You go to the kitchen and find something to eat, assuaging the hunger before returning to your desk. The hunger gestalt is completed and you start working again (pick up the unfinished gestalt of working). You have made appropriate contact with your inner experience in becoming aware of hunger and you have made appropriate contact with the environmental materials necessary to assuage the hunger and bring closure. The need is taken care of and the experience fades into the ground of life experience. The unfinished gestalt of work at your desk can then come back into focus. In another scenario, you are working and feel hunger pangs; however, because of some external demands on your time, you think you have to finish the current project and you try to ignore the hunger pangs, which increasingly intrude upon your attention to the task at hand, resulting in less productive work than would result from having no distractions. What you are left with are two unfinished gestalten emerging from need and claiming attention simultaneously. You do not appropriately make the contacts necessary to meet either need and discomfort results. You are not open to contactfulness.

ILL HEALTH

Imbalance

As action, contact, choice, and authenticity characterize health in Gestalt therapy, so stasis, resistance, rigidity, and overcontrol characterize ill health. These illness states are seen as states of psychological discomfort, often associated with anxiety. They signal some imbalance within the individual, possibly some blocking of natural functioning. The discomfort may signal some prevention of the natural assimilation of input from the environment and, thus, inhibit learning and growth.

When the organism is functioning in a natural, spontaneous, dynamic way, it responds openly to internal and external events. Energy is directed toward active participation or exchange with parts of the environment with which the individual is in contact. The contact may be aggressive or passive, assimilative or rejecting, but it is appropriate and healthy for the organism. Blocking this dynamic interaction inhibits the essential gestalt formation and completion process, encouraging unhealthy states. In the following subsection we discuss five primary ways in which ill health is manifested and encouraged: anxiety, depression, leaving business unfinished, manipulation, and denial of personal experience by introjection, projection, retroflection, deflection, and confluence. Gestalt therapy theory and practice recognizes that ill health may have a physiological base. Thus, manifestations of both anxiety and depression may be treated appropriately with other than psychological interventions.

Anxiety

The central ingredient in unhealthy and ineffective behavior is most often anxiety, the psychological state least tolerated by the human organism. The Gestalt understanding of anxiety is both simple and profound. F. Perls (1969) says that anxiety is a lack of trust in future coping ability, or in the individual's self-support system, and may be experienced as "free-floating" anxiety with no appropriate, specific target. It also may be experienced as "stage fright," specific anxiety about or concern over expected performances in the future. These events may be near (what may happen when one gets home from work) or distant (what the world will be like after a nuclear holocaust).

Fantasies about either catastrophic or anastrophic future events arouse excitement and release energy. A person may become excited in anticipation. However, often there is either no immediate appropriate outlet or the person blocks the possible actions or behaviors that are imagined; then, such imaginings generate anxiety. The energy that might go into creative action goes into obsessive thinking or other mental or physical gymnastics unrelated to either the present experience or the future.

A secretary may be excited about going home after work. If that excitement occurs early in the day, she may feel unsettled at work throughout the day. If, at some point, she remembers that her estranged boyfriend may call to discuss some unfinished business between them, she may experience increased jumpiness, lack the ability to focus on her work, or have a tendency to drop things. Anxiety is a mental jump into the future, whereas the body can exist only in the present. The anxiety, however, becomes part of the present experience of the body and influences the rest of the person's responses. Since the body is not able to react to the future, it can only react to the split that occurs between the person's body and the person's fantasies or thoughts focused on the future. So the secretary may reach for some typing paper while her thoughts are focused on the imminent confrontation with her boyfriend. Her body does not get clear signals as to how to perform and, in reaching out, she may tip over a stack of papers.

Disturbances of Contact

Growth and learning in the Gestalt model take place when there is contact—contact with the environment or contact with one or more aspects of the organism. Ideally, in adult learning we "taste" and "chew" in the process of making contact; that is, as we attend to the experience of the contact, we discriminate in order to choose to assimilate or reject that which is new to us. Such contact mandates awareness, knowledge, experience, and a sense of self as discriminatory tools. In the process of meeting needs, as we have seen in the presentation of the gestalt experience cycle (see Figure 2.1), this kind of contactful process takes place. A need arises; we scan ourselves and our environment to see how we can meet that need; we choose one of the available ways; we make contact and then we can choose to assimilate or reject that with which we have made contact.

Contact takes place at the boundary between the organism and the environment or between the organism and other part(s) of itself. The process of assimilation or rejection, of owning or disowning, of identification with or alienation from takes place at the boundary. It is in this process that we define ourselves in relation to our environment. We become clear as to what is "me" and what is "not me." As we grow, we constantly change our boundary to include new learnings and experiences. We develop new relationships, new ideas of who we are, of what we can do, and of what we believe; we also change or clarify values, attitudes, and skills. We expand our boundary. We also may reject previously held relationships, ideas, beliefs, or attitudes; in that case we contract our boundary.

Five potentially unhealthy psychological processes occur at the contact boundary: introjection, projection, retroflection, deflection, and the state of confluence. In *Gestalt Therapy* (F. Perls et al., 1951) and in F. Perls' workshop therapy, four "neurotic mechanisms" were cited as interruptions of healthy functioning: introjection, projection, retroflection, and confluence. More recent formulations (Polster and Polster, 1973) have expanded and modified that set of descriptions to include deflection. Also, confluence is now seen as a boundary disturbance as well as a state in which the distinction between self and not-self is impaired (Swanson, 1988). Each of these boundary processes is a natural function of the organism and a part of our everyday living. Each process, however, can also function to interrupt, impede, or distort organismic self-regulation. We can use these processes to block energy, protect a self-image, and distort perception, to falsify our sense of who we are or our relationship to our world. Unfinished business, anxiety, depression, fears, phobias, and other symptoms are a result of one's boundary processes. They also contribute to boundary disturbances. Thus, each of these boundary processes and states may sometimes be used to deny personal experience.

Of the five boundary processes, introjection and projection are the most basic processes used in learning, particularly in early learning. We shall discuss these first.

Introjection and Projection. To introject something is to take it in whole, to absorb it, to copy it, or to "swallow" it without reflecting upon it. The introjected element may be an idea, attitude, belief or behavior. Young children introject behavioral patterns, ways of relating, manners, basic beliefs about people, religious beliefs and practices, values, and a myriad of other phenomena. Having introjected something, such as a new word or new idea, they "try it out"; that is, they project it into their world. To project is to attribute to objects or persons in the environment the traits, attitudes, or behaviors that are actually personal. Children may use the introjected word or idea in the interaction with a parent, a friend, a dog, or a toy. Through projection in this fashion, individuals affect the world and get reactions or feedback. Based on how they experience projections and on the responses they get from the environment, they identify with or reject the introject that has been projected.

Children grow by repetitions of the process of contact, introjection, and projection. They gradually learn how to communicate, how to relate, and how to meet their own needs. They build behavior patterns and over time develop a sense of self, of who they are in relation to their world. As children, their discriminating abilities are not well developed; thus they absorb and identify with much of what they contact. As they grow from childhood to adulthood, however, they may learn to use their faculties to examine or attend to their own feelings and organismic reactions to new ideas, behaviors, religious concepts, or political attitudes, to forestall the introjection process.

Although many of the introjects from parents, siblings, school, religious instruction, television, and culture are healthy and growth producing, a significant portion of introjects are unhealthy; that is, they are in conflict with self, organism, and organismic self-regulation. For example, many children are told in obvious or subtle ways that they are bad, stupid, clumsy, sissy, or brilliant, only to find out later that these attributes are not true for them. Many also swallow biases, prejudices, attitudes, and belief systems as children, which do not fit with organismic self-regulation or self-appraisal after they become more clearly aware of who and what they are. A focus in Gestalt therapy may be the identification of introjects that are interfering with optimal functioning, their examination, and identification with or rejection of the introjected material.

The power and long-term effects of unhealthy introjects can be seen in the following example. A client, whom we shall call John, grew up in a family that taught and strictly adhered to the teaching of a church that believed people were born wicked. In addition, John's father was very rigid and strict; he punished John severely for minor deviations from the rules of the church and from the father's interpretation of those rules. At the age of 34, John was very depressed. He was extremely self-critical and, although he had moved far away from his family of origin and had rejected their church and its beliefs, he was unable to experience himself as other than "wicked to the very core." John entered therapy when he found himself yelling at his 4-year-old child with words he recognized as his father's. He had thought that he had left his father and the beliefs, values, and behaviors of his father behind, but he said, "It is as if my father is inside of me and is still running my life."

After 2 years of weekly therapy sessions, many of them spent confronting his feelings toward his father, John was much less depressed and self-critical. He reported, however, that he felt as if he needed to be constantly on guard because "my father still can pop up in my mind or come out in how I interact with my son." Powerful negative introjects such as those taken on by John from his father are not easily modified.

With introjection, individuals absorb input from outside their boundary and take it inside their boundary. With projection, they take some attitude, belief, perception, or feeling from inside and impose it on the world.

Projection may be healthy or unhealthy, accurate or distorted, functional or nonfunctional, as is true of introjection. It is by means of projection that one is able to empathize with a friend, feel sympathy for someone, identify with another person's situation, or understand someone else. All creative persons use projection to create something or to do something in a new way. Projection can also be used to deny experience, to distort a part of oneself, believing it resides in someone else. Through projection, individuals perceive the world in their own images and distort perceptions of people or events in accordance with their beliefs, attitudes, or emotions. When they perceive what they want to perceive rather than what is really there, they are projecting. When they deny their own anger, greed, manipulation, defensiveness, sexuality, caring, love, or any aspect of themselves they see in others, they are projecting.

Let us look at an example so that we may have some explicit material to use in understanding projection. In a group discussion of personal family experiences, one of the men in the group opened his mouth to make a statement. Before any words emerged, another man said, "I know what you are going to say. Your parents were not happy in their marriage." The first man responded that he had not started to say that and, furthermore, he resented having "words put in my mouth." In the subsequent discussion, the second man acknowledged that his own parents had not been happy in their marriage. He had projected his own experience into the mouth of the first man. The projective process then can be used to attribute to other people feelings, ideas, attitudes, and values that are ours. The second man in the example acknowledged that it was very difficult for him to accept the knowledge that his parents had not been happy together, thus also acknowledging his own discomfort with the situation and disowning it through projection.

Unhealthy projection is extremely common. "You must be crazy." "You can't do that." "Johnny, what are you doing? Come here at once!" Each of these statements or questions is based on some attribution of personal feelings or experiences to other persons, or represents possible personal responses to the feelings or experiences of another person that are not owned as personal. The underlying message is "If I were you, I'd feel crazy" or "I'd be unable to do that" or "If I were Johnny, I'd probably be doing something wrong." The speaker in each case is projecting a personal, world view upon someone else.

The Gestalt therapy position is phenomenological: each person construes and constructs a personal life world that is unique. Each person functions in the world on the basis of observations about which ideas, assumptions, or fantasies are constructed. No person can know how the world is for anyone else; one can only use one's projective imagination to construe it. The healthy position is to make clear observations as to what is perceived to be going on, to recognize and accept responsibility for the observations, to be aware of projecting, and to be receptive to new information. Projection without awareness, responsibility, and receptivity to new information leads to the denial of important sensory information, replacing that information with one's own ideas or fantasies.

Retroflection. Retroflection involves the redirection of energy which in healthy functioning would be directed outward into the environment for contact. Smith (1986) calls it "forms of nonenactment"—self-hate, narcissism (self-love), and self-control. In each form, the new direction is inward, as the individual does to him- or herself what would spontaneously be done to objects or persons in the environment. In self-hate, an internal process, the active part of the self aggresses against the passive part. In narcissism, the interactive healthy need to give and receive love is subverted and the energy that might go out to a target in the environment is turned back onto the self. In self-control, action toward the environment is inhibited.

In unhealthy retroflection, anger or aggression is turned back on oneself. In healthy retroflection, the individual's conscious adaptation to social norms has functional value, for it provides the sort of control that protects him/her from external threat. When individuals stop themselves from certain behaviors because their expression could result in harm to others or to self, retroflection is adaptive and functional.

Self-discipline is retroflective in the redirection of energy through choice of activity. However, if individuals unconsciously redirect suppressed impulses against themselves, this retroflection often leads to self-destructive behavior. In extreme chronic forms, retroflection becomes self-restricting, self-torture, self-martyrdom, or self-denial.

A client reports the sensation of heat or burning in an area localized under the left rib cage, although there is no physical reason for such an experience. In therapy, the heat is recognized as emanating from something that seems like a bruise. Further exploration discloses that it is the kind of bruise the client would like to inflict on a family member with whom the client is angry. The client is also afraid of that family member; thus, potentially aggressive energy has retroflected into self-aggressive energy. The client has turned the anger back on him- or herself.

Deflection. The process of contact deflection was first identified by Polster and Polster (1973). Excitement is generated when healthy contact is made with something new and nurturing. When individuals turn aside or distance themselves from healthy contact, the energy is deflected off-target. As the Polsters have pointed out, examples of deflection are multitudinous. They include avoiding eye contact, verbal circumlocutions, using generalities, excessively polite or stereotypic language, disallowing intense emotion, and talking about the past or the future instead of present experience. Both initiator and responder feel untouched or misunderstood when deflection occurs. Contact at the boundary is diffuse and weak.

The language of politics and diplomacy is full of deflections, some of which may be necessary and useful. The languages of science, business, and institutions are also full of deflections, most of which only obfuscate. These conscious deflections serve practical or political functions and may be justified under certain conditions.

In response to a threat, either real or perceived, deflections may be the avoidance strategy of choice. If a therapist makes an observation about a client's lack of eye contact and he or she responds that "all members of my family do that," direct contact is deflected. The client may continue to discuss problems of family members, unless the therapist intervenes to recall him or her to the present situation. Deflection, as an unconscious avoidance mechanism, tends to reduce the contact and to increase the isolation of individuals from others and from their own experiences.

Confluence. When we are in the state of confluence, we do not experience ourselves as being distinct from our environment; we merge into the beliefs, attitudes, and feelings that surround us (Swanson, 1988). We feel safe in our confluence with our families, our jobs, or our possessions, but our own personal experience is denied. Contact with the environment, established through clear awareness of self and not-self, is minimal. Through projection, introjection, retroflection, and deflection, the boundaries between the individual and the environment are confused and distorted. Through confluence, awareness of boundaries is seriously impaired.

One of the common confluent experiences occurs between parents and children. A father may have expectations for a son entirely out of keeping with what the son can do or wants to do. In fact, the father may not be aware of the son as a separate person; he may not experience any boundary between them. He may expect the son to be and to do just as he is and does himself. For the father, the experience is one of confluence; there is no meaningful contact with his son. The son, in this case, may also experience confluence. He claims to have the same values, attitudes, and feelings as does his father. On the other hand, if the son does not take on the parental values and injunctions, the relationship is likely to be disturbed or conflicted; there may be little or no understanding of one another.

In another context, confluence can be positive, an essential part of what Maslow (1962) calls a "peak experience," a moment of "highest happiness and fulfillment." In the peak experiences, cognition of Being or B-cognition (in Maslow's terms) takes over; the object perceived is not seen as one figure against a background from which it is distinguished; rather, there is no awareness of anything but the object perceived, no sense of differentiation from it, no perception of it as "something to be used or something to be afraid of, or to be reacted to in some other human way." Such cognition is of Being, of wholeness. A common example is the merging felt in intimate lovemaking. Confluence, in this context, is an intensely rich, "ego-transcending, self-forgetful, egoless" experience. An I-Thou experience in therapy may have these qualities. Such peak experiences are momentary happenings; they cannot be planned or engineered. In the normal day-to-day reality of living in the world, the unhealthy confluent experience is not "selfless" but is the absence of necessary boundaries between the self and aspects of the environment.

Since confluent individuals cannot be extricated from surroundings with which they have merged, the development of projections, introjections, retroflections, and deflections are more likely to occur. The necessary discriminatory perceptions that distinguish what is perceived as "self" from what is "not-self" have been subverted. Unhealthy confluence, then, is the most insidious of the five inhibitors of growth we have discussed.

Manipulation

Manipulation works in two ways, both of which are unhealthy. The individual may lack self-support and, in order to cope with the life situation, learns to manipulate the environment, the self, or both. We shall discuss each of these phenomena in the following paragraphs.

Manipulation of the Environment. The discussion of healthy processes in the first section of this chapter suggests that maturity and responsibility entail the individual's ability and willingness to generate self-support rather than to be dependent upon support from others. In this context, manipulation is using one's energies to obtain and maintain support from the environment rather than generating support from within.

If a person does not generate the necessary psychological self-support and experiences anxiety in dealing with environmental impact, that person may attempt to manipulate others into providing the necessary support. Manipulation, then, becomes an inappropriate, yet pervasive, strategy for satisfying perceived needs. In Gestalt therapy, this strategy is believed to be a manifestation of ill health.

To avoid or reduce anxiety, people often develop complex manipulative behavior that to them may seem the only way of satisfying personal needs, but which in reality heightens their dependent behavior and separates them from healthy self-support. If an individual knows no effective way to reduce the anxiety that dominates his or her experience, any actions that seem to alleviate anxiety, even temporarily, are adopted.

After considering the ways of denying personal experience, it becomes easy to imagine a community dominated by a complicated web of manipulative patterns, as person after person develops manipulative styles for dealing with self or others in order to find satisfaction that is not self-generated. Such a scenario is, in fact, implied in the writings of F. Perls, who sees few authentically healthy members of society. In Gestalt therapy, it is believed that, to the extent an individual is manipulative, he or she is neurotic.

Let us assume here that all persons are neurotic to some extent, that is, manipulative of environments for support or affirmation of feelings of self-worth. Environments rarely provide all of the other persons or experiences, the richness and possibilities, or the support and challenge needed to satisfy individual needs. Western-culture institutions have developed in the bureaucratic model in which the goal is largely to preserve the institutions rather than to care for the needs of individual members of society (Berger, Berger, and Kellner, 1973). It is often necessary, even for healthy persons, to learn how to manipulate effectively in order to survive in unsupportive environments. The distinction we make is that neurotics are unaware of their manipulations and the effect of such manipulations on themselves. Healthy persons may knowingly choose manipulative behavior when it serves them in their effort to achieve satisfactory closure.

F. Perls (1969) suggests that the neurotic expects from the therapist those things not forthcoming from the environment. In other words, in the therapeutic environment, a client will use the manipulative, dependency-oriented behavior learned from the external environment. The therapist, however, refuses to provide the support gained manipulatively elsewhere. When the therapist provides unnecessary support, further dependence is encouraged, thus preventing a neurotic client from reaching a level of self-support that permits him or her to give up the unconscious and self-defeating manipulation of others (Resnick, 1975).

Manipulation of Self. Individuals may manipulate themselves as well as their environments. They may pay attention to certain aspects of their own experience and ignore or avoid others. They may over-identify with certain characteristics and create rigid, uncompromising, prejudicial attitudes toward the self.

One common way of manipulating the self to stay blocked from healthy contact with the environment is the self-torture game labeled by F. Perls as "topdog vs. underdog." The top dog aspect of the personality is the demander-of-perfection, the manifestation of a set of introjected "shoulds" and "shouldn'ts": "I should be on time, I should keep my house clean and neat at all times, I should never talk back to my boss, I should never be angry, I should always do perfect work. . . ." The top dog, speaking only to the individual from within, is an introjection of societal, familial, or authoritarian demands. Opposed to the top dog is the underdog, the manifestation of resistance to external demands. Essentially, the underdog agrees that the top dog's demands are appropriate; however, the underdog's internal sabotage assures that the demands will never be met: "I'll never be able to be on time, I'll never be able to do everything right, poor me, I'll always be neurotic."

The underdog (victim) aspect of the psyche experiences the world as a threat, as a fearful place, and develops coping strategies necessary to manage the fear. Such strategies may include hostility, passive-aggression, obsessiveness, and compulsiveness. Incipient fear may grow into paranoia. Two aspects of the personality often arise from the underdog stance: when the world is inhospitable, the child may find the center of his or her world to be the self and narcissism becomes the coping mechanism; or, without the stabilizing influence of good, validating contact with at least one significant other, the childish sense of identity does not coalesce; the core gestalten relating to self-definition may not merge or may remain unfinished.

The defenses for psychological survival learned as a child persist through later years as chronic and habitual responses that become one of the primary targets during therapy. They effectively block both the emergence of a positive self-image and the life energy that must be released to fuel the radiance, excitement, centeredness, and contactfulness of real living.

Leaving Gestalten Incomplete

The main source of discomfort for most people is what Gestalt therapists call unfinished business. For example, when one feels hurt, angry, or resentful toward another person and does not resolve those feelings in some way—expressing them or letting them go—the experience is incomplete. By holding on to unfinished experiences or avoiding closure in any way, a person invests available energy and emotional reserves in sustaining the incompleteness, leaving little energy available for encountering new situations and assimilating the gestalten of continuing experiences. The psychological processes are these: the dominant need surfaces in the person's awareness; the dominant need is to complete a gestalt; the person does not do what is needed to accomplish the completion; then, either the unfinished situation will continue to emerge into awareness as an image or a tension in some part of the body or the person will set up some kinds of controls to accommodate to the sense of incompleteness. The tension may become so chronic the person is no longer aware of it. The person rehearses mentally over and over what might have been said or done; the body becomes armored against chronic threat.

These controls take great amounts of energy to maintain—energy not available for healthy contacts in the present. A person's effectiveness in responding to new experiences and his or her availability for new experiences that can be encountered are limited. Since the organism's primary motivation is to achieve closure, what emerges as figure is business that is not completed unless the organism uses some countertherapeutic measures to control awareness or responses.

Unfinished business consists primarily of past relationships or intrapsychic conflicts that have not been resolved. Some examples of unfinished situations are unexpressed resentment or anger toward parents, siblings, lovers, and spouses; or unexpressed love, unresolved guilt, unaccepted past actions. The lack of resolution may involve other persons or aspects of oneself. When persons do not act in ways necessary for closure, do not forgive actions that have happened in the past, or do not accept situations as they are, they are unable to function healthily and energetically.

Sometimes the tension of maintaining the unfinished business is covert; that is, it is buried in psychological defenses that are hidden from awareness so that the nature of the tension may be masked. Sometimes the tension finds expression in the body, as shown by Rolf (1977), Lowen (1967), and Reich (1949), through such psychosomatic complaints as ulcers, tension headaches, lower back pain, arthritis, or asthma attack.

Psychological defenses, such as conversations in absentia, may be rehearsals for the actual interactions. By rehearsing, an individual is either trying to change the past or planning expressions and reactions for the future. This kind of effort may extend as far as rehearsing a complete dialogue by imagining the other person's responses or statements. Imagining conversations constitutes one of the primary means used by the individual in an attempt to reduce anxiety related to expectations about the future. In reality, the anxiety is continued or even exacerbated by the imaginings.

This is not to minimize the possibly therapeutic nature of such rehearsals in a therapy session in which the individual deals with unfinished gestalten. (See Appendix A for an example.) Such techniques will be described in the next chapter. It is to say that unfinished business buried in some kind of bodily distress is also unproductive and unhealthy. Unfinished business, thus, becomes an impediment to seeing and experiencing things as they are.

Depression

In the earlier formulations of Gestalt therapy, presented in the first edition of this book, anxiety was viewed as the primary neurotic mechanism. Today's understanding is that depression is just as insidious and debilitating as anxiety.

Whereas in anxiety the energies go outward in seemingly uncontrolled and chaotic fashion, the depressed person generally feels the energy as heavy, dark, and pulling downward as if flowing with the force of gravity. Depression is a multifaceted phenomenon related to blocking healthy completion of gestalten when appropriate expression is denied. Several different phenomena tend to be lumped into this one category; some are legitimate healthy responses to experience, whereas some are retroflexive responses and generate ill health. When labeled depression, all are experienced as problems; depression is a pejorative term in Western culture. For example, grief is often labeled depression although it is a legitimate life experience of reaction to loss. Tiredness or exhaustion may be labeled depression and treated as illness when what is most needed is withdrawal for rest.

Retroflexive depression is depression resulting when energy that needs to go out toward the environment is thwarted; it signals ill health. Anger retroflected into the individual may be experienced as depression. Love that is not expressed may be felt as depression. Any neurotic mechanisms that block real contact, such as a sense of powerlessness, may have depression as a concomitant. True living is experienced when contacts with the self and the environment are clear and allowed to proceed unobstructed. Each new experience is a meeting. When these meetings are obstructed, the energy that might be expended in healthy contact is depressed.

The experience of depression is a signal that some process either within the individual or between the individual and the environment is malfunctioning. These signals may emerge as manifestations of the inner motivation toward health. One female client reported feelings of depression (a dark and heavy downward pull in her solar plexus area) that signaled the possibility she was planning to do something that would not be good for her. A male client experienced depression in connection with going to a job for which he discovered an unacknowledged dislike and dissatisfaction. Adolescent depression often signals the fact that the healthy need for significant interaction with self and others has been blocked. The motivation toward health uses whatever signals may serve to alert the individual to a need for a change.

SUMMARY

In this chapter, we have presented value-oriented definitions of good and ill health from the Gestalt therapy perspective. Health is experienced through the gestalt formation and completion process; it actualizes one's own inner set of values, wisdom, power, and love; develops one's own inner support system; enables the individual to value and to manifest awareness, wholeness, responsibility, and authenticity; and it enables the individual to have good, lively contact with self and with the environment. That which promotes ill health blocks, impedes, avoids, or interrupts the gestalt formation and completion process resulting in anxiety, depression, or both; values stasis, resistance to change, rigidity, and neurotic control; involves attempts to manipulate the environment for self-definition and support; denies personal experience through the psychological mechanisms of projection, introjection, retroflection, deflection, and confluence, each of which, when used in unhealthy ways, encourages lack of clarity in boundaries and contact functions necessary for healthy interaction with the environment. Maturation is the process of moving from reliance on manipulating the environment for support to becoming self-sustaining and self-supportive.

Chapter 4

The Change Process and the Course of Therapy

THE CHANGE PROCESS

Given the psychological and psychodynamic foundations explained in the first two chapters and the definitions of good and ill health in chapter 3, one may conclude that the simplest, most basic way to change and grow is through organismic self-regulation and conscious choice in a continuous interaction between the organism and the environment. Growth and change, in this case, happen in an effortless process of recognition of organismic needs—awareness of incomplete gestalten—and selection of actions that will meet the needs—complete the gestalten—and allow free movement to the next need that arises.

Consider a hypothetical woman who is at home one afternoon when, in a telephone call from her husband, she learns he is bringing one of his clients home for dinner. The woman looks around the house with the awareness that it looks pretty messy. She thinks that the dinner she has planned is not very elegant, although there will be enough food for an extra person. The woman takes a deep breath, straightens the house, prepares what she has available in the best way possible, dresses herself as nicely as she can, and is prepared to meet the guest. This woman deals with emerging needs as she is aware of them, dealing with each by choosing materials and activities from what she has available, moving from housekeeping to dinner preparation and dressing as efficiently as possible.

Consider another woman confronted with the same situation. This woman is filled with anxiety as soon as she hears her husband's voice. Because of inner conflicts that emerge regarding this event, she is unable to think clearly or to work effectively, and is not ready when the guest arrives. She ends by feeling totally distraught. She is angry at both her husband and herself, is full of blame, and is making acrimonious charges. She has a terrible headache and an upset stomach. All of the gestalten are incomplete.

Consider a man who goes to the office feeling good, takes care of each situation as it arises in an appropriate fashion, is authentically positive in these circumstances, who goes home at the end of the day and takes care of home business and pleasure appropriately, who goes to bed and sleeps soundly. Consider another man who goes to the office fearful, controls himself all day in order to try to behave appropriately, and then goes home exploding with negativity that is vented on anyone or anything he may encounter.

Few of us are able to trust our organismic functioning, allowing ourselves to meet needs with whatever materials and actions are available, as did the first man and woman in our illustrations. Most people have learned how not to live fully and completely, how to interfere with healthy, self-regulatory gestalt formation-completion processes and contact. Most people have learned how to create unrest in their lives. From the Gestalt perspective, however, we begin with the assumption that all persons who come into therapy by choice have the ingredients necessary to live, grow, and change in ways beneficial to them. They have learned how not to do that, how to block the self-regulatory processes, how to ignore needs, how to live with incomplete gestalten and with the anxiety, depression, or discomfort that is a consequence of such incompleteness.

Many people who behave as the second man or woman did in our illustration may eventually come into therapy wanting some sort of change. They may say, "I have this problem I want to solve," or "I'm having trouble with my husband who insists on bringing guests home to dinner at the last moment," or "I'm having trouble with my boss who overloads me with work," or "I'm having a problem with my girlfriend, boyfriend, son, father, mother," or "I'm having a problem with myself."

From the Gestalt point of view, such problems are a set of undesirable consequences of behaviors of oneself or of others. In the therapeutic situation, the environmental aspects of any client's "problems" cannot be dealt with unless the situation is restructured to include significant others; however the boss, father, mother, child, husband, wife, or job is not present. The reality of the environmental conditions cannot be ascertained. What is present is a client with the perceptions, feelings, thoughts, memories, images, and behaviors that have been activated by the environment, and those perceptions constitute the world as the client believes it to be. In Gestalt therapy, the client is the focus of interest; what that client does with inner experiences related to external conditions can be explored.

Our second woman from the first illustration may say, "I can't cope with my home life any longer. I have a constant stomachache and headaches, and I explode at the slightest provocation." The focus in therapy is that she copes by getting stomachaches, headaches, and exploding; she has learned to behave in those ways; these are her patterns of response to her home environment. She has alternatives. She may continue to behave in the customary way; she may blame her husband—if he were different everything would be fine. This may, in fact, be true. The husband, however, is not in therapy. She is. Therefore, another alternative is to look at her own behavior in an effort to understand what she does and how she does it, so that she may discover other possibilities for herself. When she understands what she does and how she does it, she has the option of making changes.

In opposition to some other therapy approaches, a client in Gestalt therapy is usually not asked why she does what she does. Reasons given for behavior are usually rationalizations, and asking *why* the client does something may not elicit insight that facilitates change. With the understanding of what she does and how she does it, the client can take responsibility for her own behavior; she can choose to change her behavior and the attendant consequences will also change. She may also discover why she has developed the neurotic patterns.

The Process Orientation

In Gestalt therapy, two kinds of change are assumed: change within the person in attitudes, feelings, behaviors, demands, or expectations, and change in the environment. Change in the environment comes outside the purview of therapy; the focus is on the client. The therapist assumes that the client has all of the tools required to make any needed or wanted personal changes. The therapist facilitates the client's discovery of what the client is doing, how he or she is doing it, and explores the dynamic processes underlying the behaviors that are a part of the presenting "problem." The therapist facilitates the client's acceptance of responsibility for the client's behavior, not for the situation or for the behaviors of others. The therapist works with the client in choosing from possible alternatives and in accepting responsibility for the choices that are made.

Within that set of seemingly simple statements is the Gestalt perspective regarding therapy: Underlying the client's problem is a personal dynamic process—an attitude, a value, a belief, a perspective, or a psychological set—that has been introjected and that defines the client's personal involvement. In order to be effective, therapeutic changes must involve that underlying psychological mechanism. In the case of Woman Two in our earlier illustration, her underlying process might be an inner demand that she be "perfect," and then her own anxiety as she tries to meet this demand for perfection and her depression when she fails.

The Paradoxical Nature of Change

Change is paradoxical in the Gestalt approach. Beisser (1970) has pointed it out: one can change only when one is truly oneself. When we are fully what we really are, we open the possibility of making changes. Attempts to deny or suppress elements of ourselves lead to self-defeating mechanisms and rigidity of behavior. F. Perls suggested that it is futile to attempt self-improvement in the way that most people mean it. If a person is constantly trying to improve, that person is focusing on a gestalt about "trying" that will never be finished. That person changes only by stopping the attempts at improvement and by allowing him- or herself to be exactly what he or she is, thus opening the way to confront unfinished gestalten. The only way unfinished gestalten may be completed is by affirming the truth, no matter what it is.

For a moment, let us compare the paradoxical theory of change with a famous paradox proposed by Zeno. According to Zeno, an arrow speeding on its way to a target does not move, because at any one instant of time the arrow is motionless. An instant is the eternal present, the moment of no movement; therefore, as life is a succession of instants, the arrow is motionless. Yet is still hits the target. The paradox comes from dividing time into segments so small that it gives the appearance of having stopped; yet in actuality, time does not stop, and the arrow is moving in the context of time moving.

Likewise, to be totally what one is at any time does not negate the change that occurs through time. Persons can be only what they are. When they are totally in the present, they do not have a sense of change and yet, they are changing. This seeming contradiction or paradox comes from the superimposition of two contexts, the momentary and the ongoing, on the notion of change.

Change Processes in Therapy

Now let us look at the kind of change that is targeted in Gestalt therapy. The client who comes into therapy with a problem experiences confusion or conflict, depression or anxiety. Although the client may experience the unpleasant feelings as an aspect of relationships with parts of the environment, the Gestalt therapist assumes that the confusion or conflict is also intrapsychic. Given Gestalt therapy's phe-nomenological assumptions as a basis to build on, the perspective is that each person generates unique personal constructs about the world, and each person behaves according to personally held ideas about the world and people in it. Therefore, the conflicts, confusions, depres-sion, or anxiety can be resolved by dealing with the client alone. Often the conflicts and confusions are not overt. The client may not recognize or acknowledge the battles being fought internally, but may actually be experiencing some form of battle fatigue from the intrapsychic con-flicts.

The target for change is not the problem presented by the client. Rather, the Gestalt therapist observes the client as he or she describes the problem and looks for underlying processes by which the client maintains the inner state of confusion, conflict, depression, or anxiety. Gertrude Krause (1977) describes this therapeutic stance cogently:

> All I do is attend. . . . I attempt to discover what the client is DOING. I am interested in that more than in the CONTENT of what he is telling me. "DOING" includes how he is sitting, breathing, are there any ob-vious tensions in his body, how he is speaking, what is the tone of his voice, his speech patterns, etc. I do not try to cover all of these points simultaneously but, as I attend, some process or processes exhibiting what he is doing become apparent. If no clues of process emerge from his presence alone, or how he expresses himself, I probably will discover what he is doing within the situation he is describing (1977, p. 2).

Discovering the underlying process or theme related to a present prob-lem is attempted on a verbal level by Bandler and Grinder (1975). Us-ing a transformational grammar perspective, these authors detail the work of the therapist in discovering the "deep structure" beneath the verbal statements by facilitating the completion of sentences in the ver-bal presentation. For example, a client may say, "It makes me angry." The *it* in the sentence has no clear referent; we do not know what *it* may be in the client's story. The therapist helps the client to complete the sentence by adding a clear subject: "My roommate makes me an-gry." In working through the verbalizations, the client comes, at last, to a personally responsible statement: "I become angry with my room-mate when she uses my things without asking permission." Within the deep, i.e., unspoken, structure are components that must be dealt with, if the therapeutic change is to take place.

The next aspect of the change process is this: simply talking about an issue or a deep conflict or depression will not complete the gestalt being focused on. Such completion comes only from experiencing, al-lowing oneself to feel, say, or do whatever is necessary for the unfin-ished business to be finished. As F. Perls says, "Gestalt therapy is an

experiential therapy, rather than a verbal or an interpretive therapy"
(1973, p. 64). The client is facilitated in saying clearly what needs to be
said, not to any real person in his or her life but to his or her image of
that person. The client is facilitated in allowing herself or himself to
experience whatever feelings, thoughts, or actions have been blocked,
thus completing the gestalt in which the unexperienced feelings have
been trapped. F. Perls notes this aspect of therapy as the "Here and
Now" component. Krause sees it as "the current process—what is the
person doing at this moment. . . . If [the client] is worrying about
something that might happen next week, his here and now is WOR-
RYING about the future" (Krause, 1977, p. 3).

The last component of the Gestalt therapy change process that we
shall deal with here is called the "I-Thou" experience. The therapist
participates freely and personally in the therapeutic encounter as a catalyst, frustrator, or clarifier, not as a familial support. The therapist
creates the "safe emergency" in which therapy may occur. A goal in
Gestalt therapy is to increase the client's self-support system. Therefore, any advice giving or problem solving is generally counter-productive. The Gestalt therapist communicates radical respect for every aspect of the client—the top dog, the underdog, the pattern of resistances,
etc. The therapist assumes the ability of the client to generate self-support, and communicates that assumption and belief by a lack of familial
support. However, when a client exhibits a general lack of self-support, a therapeutic caring stance may be appropriate. The skill of the
therapist is indicated by the way in which the client's frustration is
balanced with the way the therapist attends to the client and the respect and caring communicated.

Change Processes: Internal and External

Change through personal choice will not occur until people accept
what is in the present, since verbal responses, modes of action, and
habitual ways of perceiving and organizing beliefs often are means of
avoiding awareness. Gestalt therapy interrupts the individual's usual
coping styles. Once attention is directed toward the awareness of actions, thoughts, intentions, and desires, the therapist directs the client
toward a level of knowledge that permits personal choice. The therapist reinforces the client for changing behaviors that block growth and,
in that way, the therapist functions as an agent for behavioral as well
as attitude change. Attempting to control, predict, change, or shape an
individual's total behavior is an overwhelming task; thus, it is more

common for behaviorally oriented therapists to select small, isolated bits of behavior that are susceptible to external control.
ion in the here-and-now. Out of this confrontation with unfinished havior externally, we can approach the problem from the internal perspective. Once we look at behavior as the external realization of people's perceptions of themselves and their world, we can help them alter their own behavior as they choose by helping them to become more aware of their own feelings and beliefs. In this way, people are assumed to have freedom of choice and to be responsible for themselves and how they behave within their personal context.

The contemporary development of an interactionist approach to describing human behavior (Bandura, 1977) states that behavior, intrapersonal characteristics, and environmental factors interact with each other. This interaction of three elements can be studied with a view toward understanding the relative strength of each factor in human life. While a behaviorist, taking an external perspective, may emphasize the relationship between environment and behavior, the Gestalt therapist emphasizes personal awareness as the most significant factor. In fact, Gestalt therapy's emphasis on personal awareness focuses the therapy process on personal factors, freedom, responsibility, and choice.

Within the Gestalt model, people are facilitated in becoming aware of themselves and of their ways of performing; thus they increase their ability to choose among several alternative behaviors and, thereby, become responsible for whatever they choose to do. A lack of self-knowledge is seen as an avoidance, controlled by the individual's unwillingness to accept some personal experiences or elements of behavior, which do not conform to his or her existing conceptions of self. In its simplest terms, this avoidance leads toward what appears to the individual to be a positive end, the maintenance of existing beliefs about the self.

In Gestalt therapy sessions, the therapist will often direct the individual's attention to some particular exhibited behavior. When individuals become aware of significant behavior that heretofore has been unknown, they can gain from that knowledge. Gestalt therapy has little interest in producing intellectual "insights," which often have the effect of reinforcing the existing behavior. The Gestalt approach encourages the individual first to observe behavior and then to re-experience it directly. Re-experiencing it brings it to the surface, so that the individual can then deal with it directly.

An important role of the therapist in the Gestalt model is to direct awareness toward what the individual is doing to block self-expression of feelings, thinking, or expression. Since the neurotic is characterized as being blind to the obvious, presenting the client with occasions for focusing on obvious behavior is, in effect, organizing an opportunity to control one's own contingencies. Gestalt therapy, like several other therapies, gives the individual reason to observe behavior, and offers methods for observing, knowing, choosing, and being in charge of it.

THE COURSE OF THERAPY

Steps in Maturation

In the course of therapy, a client matures by making transitions from using unhealthy strategies that attempt to manipulate the environment for support to using healthy processes in contacts with others. Five process steps and one underlying change seem to be necessary (Korb, 1984). We use the image of steps because it suggests both the idea of a pause between activities, to focus on a somewhat defined area, and the idea of movement to and from such an area. The steps suggested here are underlying gestalten with beginnings, developments, endings, and transitions; when unfinished, these gestalten are not discrete; thus the mix of material is complex at all times. Clients do not move easily through the steps. Beginnings and backtracks, movements forward, backward, and sometimes sideways may be made as clients relate their experiences between sessions or as material emerges in a particular session. Each client's process of figure formation out of the ground of his or her experience is unique.

Step 1: Focus on Present Behavior. At the start of therapy, clients present their awareness of confusion, frustration, anxiety, or depression regarding some specific behaviors, either their own or the behaviors of others that have been disturbing. "I am not doing well in my job," or "I am not sleeping well," or "My friends tell me I need some help because I am driving them crazy" are typical behavioral reports. Since what the client presents is the starting point for therapy, current behaviors become the first target. However, the look at the current behavior very soon, sometimes almost immediately, leads to . . .

Step 2: Focus on Old Business. Present problem behaviors are often signals or repetitions of behaviors learned as survival mechanisms in times of turmoil. These behaviors may reveal an automatic anger response to frustration, a clenching of a fist or a jaw, a blocking of a visual or auditory perception. During traumatic experiences in childhood, when children's coping strategies with significant persons in their environment are inadequate, some survival response is made that pushes that trauma into the ground of the life experience. Perhaps my father glared at me every time I spoke too loudly. I learned to tighten my throat muscles to prevent myself from yelling or speaking in a loud tone so that I would not trigger his disapproval. The response itself, the tightening of the throat muscles, is then habitually repeated in later situations in which there is any possibility of being glared at. In a sense, the child who fears being glared at gets "stuck" at that traumatic point and does not grow or change in that aspect (G. Krause, personal communication, April, 1971). Gestalten from the past are left unfinished.

Achieving closure on unfinished gestalten from the past is the essential task that emerges when such survival mechanisms are questioned. For example, awareness of the clenching of a jaw may lead to awareness of hurt and anger that have been buried. Affirmation of the hurt and anger through experiencing them in therapy brings closure. This kind of therapeutic work clarifies the contact boundary with the environment, freeing this contact system to function in a healthy fashion in the here-and-now. Out of this confrontation with unfinished business and the completion of gestalten also comes . . .

Step 3: Focus on a Core Self-Concept. Buried under the hurt and anger, the sadness, the frustration, or the deadness that signals unfinished business from the past is a kind of early learning (a compilation of the early introjects) about the self, a self-concept. Without exception, this concept is pejorative and self-denigrating: "I can't do anything right," "I am not lovable," "I don't deserve anything good," "I have to control everything around me or I won't succeed." Clarity about this core concept and affirmation of its relevance to the client's experience are essential to reach closure on early learnings. What emerges next for the client is attention to the present and . . .

Step 4: Focus on Life Decision Making. A successful transition to self-support is based on clients making decisions to engage actively in the creation of their lives. Environments such as families or work settings often demand subservience: "Don't give me hassles," "Don't be yourself, be what I want you to be" is the institutional message. However, human beings need to feel alive, to be vitally engaged in the business of living (Lifton, 1976). A decision must be made to honor the vitality within; this is a life-affirming decision, which is the key to recovery from any kind of debilitation.

Clients who come for therapy evidence a will to live by inserting themselves into a therapeutic process. However, clients also may have a self-defeating mechanism involved in the key self-concept, extending sometimes as far as a suicidal mechanism. To reach the self-supportive stage, clients must decide, sometimes more than once, in favor of living the life that has been given to them, in the body that has been given, with the talents that have been given, in the world the way it is with ups and downs, ins and outs, constant changes, and endemic stresses. This decision is sometimes made in an intense, overt intrapsychic confrontation; sometimes the decision is covert and surfaces in the client's behavior, attention, and energy patterns. However it happens, clients who become self-supportive turn a corner at some point into life affirmation and from then on what emerges in therapy is . . .

Step 5: Focus on New Behavior. As the core concept from the past becomes clear and the will to live is evidenced, clients begin to deal with new issues or with the original presenting problem or experience in a new light. "If this is who I am and this is life as it comes to me, what does it mean to live, not just to exist? What does it mean for me? What choices do I want to make?" In this step, old issues often emerge but with new insights and clarity. New issues are often dealt with tentatively and with caution.

The length of time spent profitably in confronting new behaviors, after becoming clear about key processes and making clear choices to live, suggests that there is an underlying change process all clients undergo: developing a new belief system. Cutting across the whole of the maturational process is the death of the old set of beliefs about the self as being insufficient, unworthy, and dependent. These beliefs are introjects or survival defenses against old, intolerable environmental conditions. In other words, the client presides over the death of core constructs about the dependent self.

Zinker (1977), following Maslow (1962), has pointed out that therapeutic work must deal with meta-needs: The need to be, to be respected and valued by a significant other, the need to be respected and valued by oneself, the need to live a life that is meaningful to oneself, the need to know and to actualize one's own truth. When not met, such needs lead to "soul sickness."

The healing of this sickness leads to the emergence of a new set of beliefs about the self as worthy, lovable, and capable. The client may still experience unfulfilled needs but does not feel as dependent on the approval of others, since the client has developed a self-supportive self-concept. In this metamorphosis, the client's "natural self" (Guntrip, 1969) containing the individual's true potential is released. These true possibilities for love, satisfaction, meaning, energy, commitment, and congruence are latent in each person and are a part of the self that emerges as a client transcends the old limited belief system.

Successful clients experience the limits of the old belief system by which they had lived. Additionally, they experience an impasse as each limit is reached; with the therapist's help they mobilize awareness, energy, and commitment for transcendence. "I can't do anything right" becomes "I can do some things well and other things not so well." "I am not okay" becomes "I am myself." "Everyone else is more important than I am" becomes "I am important and I believe in myself."

Perhaps the critical element in the process of metamorphosis, and the one that takes the longest, is learning to trust the self-supportive mechanisms, learning that there is wisdom in the organism that can be known and counted on, and learning to believe in that wisdom. Such trust grows through experimentation, both in and out of therapy, and takes considerable time, sometimes years.

An Extended Example of the Process of Maturation

The client whose experience we use as a primary illustration of the maturational steps is Art, an astute, intelligent, personable professor in his early 40s. He was referred to one of the authors by a mutual friend. His presenting problem was that he had had four marriages behind him and found himself repeating past performance with the woman he was presently seeing. His frustration had reached a critical mass, so to speak. In therapy, Art worked through the present behaviors (Step 1) and past marital experiences to the point of clarity about their roots in early experiences in his family and his early relationships with females. The unfinished issues related to these experiences surfaced slowly (Step 2) and were clarified during about 2 years of intermittent, intense therapeutic encounters.

An underlying process emerged during this time (Step 3): from his parents and early conservative community contacts, Art had learned "categories" (his words) of behaviors and feelings that explained right and wrong types of relationships between the sexes. These categories were well-established by the time he was 16. In each marriage, when he encountered behaviors that contradicted or were not explained by his categories of rightness, he divorced and moved on. When he decided to go into therapy, he was determined to look at himself in his relationships, even though the look was disconcerting and often painful. In one of the pivotal sessions, Art saw his categories clearly, saw where they had come from, saw they were no longer useful, looked at the therapist, and said:

"But I believed in them. What do I believe now?"

"What do you have left?"

"There's just me," he said. "And I don't believe in me very much." (Step 3)

At that point, Art began to make explicit statements of what he did believe (the underlying change process in action). There were more statements than he had anticipated. His emerging belief in himself and beliefs about himself were actually substantial. He was a capable person, a loving person, a perceptive person, an intelligent person, and an ethical person with his own experiences of right and wrong. He made these statements tentatively and cautiously, but with a growing sense of their truth.

Following this session, Art and the therapist continued to meet for many months to deal with his current experiences (Step 5). Some of the work focused on old behavioral patterns and the old self-concept, showing their inappropriateness for the present; some work focused on the need for new behaviors and new thought patterns. Currently, he is still learning to trust his own perceptions and judgments, rather than the old learned categories of right and wrong.

Art never overtly confronted the life decision we have noted as Step 4. His decision for life seems to have been made before he came to therapy, and was reinforced as he experienced his own energy renewal and the enlivening of his relationships with others and with himself.

Further Examples of Maturation

Art's experience is only one example of the maturational processes. His experience in therapy substantially followed the steps outlined. However, other clients who have worked to the self-supportive stage have not done so. Emma, for example, discovered her key self-concept early. By the age of 4 she had learned from her mother that "I'll never be able to do anything right," and she spent her life proving that her mother's estimation of her was accurate. She set herself up for failure. Emma worked on the first three steps almost simultaneously.

Ann, on the other hand, spent more than a year in Step 1. Ann had so little self-support when she entered therapy that she could be physically out of control and could faint when trying to walk alone into a room that had no chairs or other persons to lean on. Ann's key concept emerged as "I have no right to care for myself when others need help." She became aware of this belief system very early in therapy and used that information as support while she worked slowly and painfully through other steps. Neither Emma nor Ann has been seen professionally for several years.

Clients experience Step 4, the life decision step, in a variety of ways. While Art seemed to have made a decision for life before he came to therapy, Paul had a very different experience. Paul came to therapy depressed and anxious. After he had spent many months confronting some intensely painful business with his parents (both dead), he came to a session and reported that he didn't know what had happened, but he had awakened that day feeling light, clear, and energetic. What filled his mind were thoughts and ideas about his work and his current relationship. He never needed to confront his self-destructive energy directly and overtly.

Beverly also spent months in therapy directly confronting her intrapsychic suicidal side. She became acquainted with this side, learning how she functioned both for and against herself, finally making a conscious choice to give her attention and her energy to her life-oriented inner side. For Beverly and many others, the decision for life is made consciously. The decision is a part of the process of "suffering one's death and being reborn" that underlies all five steps of the maturational process.

The examples mentioned above suggest the vast range of possibilities, in the work with individuals, so far as content, language, concept, image, and every other facet of the client's therapeutic experience are concerned. Whatever the client's needs, the steps toward maturation are usually made slowly and with difficulty.

In addition to the possibility that some clients may skip one or more steps in the process, a further complication is that several levels of gestalten are being confronted almost simultaneously. A client may explore unfinished business related to life events, to perceptions, to past life events, and to beliefs and self-concepts at the same time. Out of this rich mix, the emerging figure for each therapeutic encounter joins with the need system of the client. For some clients, these sets of gestalten seem to occur in somewhat structured levels, with self-concepts at the core. For other clients, the figure that emerges at each session may relate to different gestalten without much obvious connecting structure. As the therapeutic work continues, however, the self-concept is either challenged or created. Such a self is not fixed or static, however (Kelly, 1963; Combs and Snygg, 1959). Changes in the most central beliefs occur slowly.

Impasse work with clients emerges not once but many times. For example, each time Art moved into work with new material, representing a new step or a new aspect of a step, an impasse emerged. Each impasse signaled a move beyond the known, and involved slow and careful steps into the unknown. Art had to test each new step for support, while attending to the need for the old and familiar. The more important the work to the core self-concept, the more active and intense is the client's involvement in the work and the slower and more careful the therapeutic work needs to be.

What seems to be triggered in the intense impasse is a survival-related fear, the kind of fear that prompted the early self-defeating, self-denigrating beliefs and behaviors. For some clients, transcendence necessitates a confrontation with the fear as a personal force. Some clients confront a symbol of fear, such as a deep dark cavern, emptiness behind a closed door, or a whirling chaos in the trunk of the body. Some clients do not need to confront the fear; nonetheless, fear motivates their impasse work.

Style in the Therapeutic Encounter

Gestalt therapy has been noted by some critics as being inappropriate for some kinds of clients: it has been alleged to be good for white, upper-class intellectuals but not for persons of different cultures or of less inner strength. These criticisms would seem to be based on an assumption that Gestalt therapy as exhibited by F. Perls in taped workshop seminars is Gestalt therapy. In the Gestalt community itself, therapists have struggled to affirm other therapeutic styles and less abrasive and confrontative behaviors. Laura Perls, who, with a group of others including her husband Fritz, began the development of Gestalt therapy more than 40 years ago and is an eminent therapist and founder of the New York Institute for Gestalt Therapy, has said that Fritz's method, using the hot seat, works well in demonstration workshops but is not appropriate for a whole therapy. In on-going therapeutic relationships with clients, more support is essential.

In actuality, F. Perls himself spoke of the "safe emergency" as the psychological arena where therapy is done. Each client's needs for safety and trust must be recognized at the same time the therapist is aware of the need to confront neurotic dependency mechanisms: another paradox in the process. F. Perls also has said that the growth process takes time. He and his wife Laura were and are much opposed to instant "cures" or "instant turn-ons." Gestalt therapy, then, builds upon a recognition and respect for all clients just as they present themselves. Since unhealthy defensive strategies are learned for personal survival reasons, they deserve respect from the therapist.

Some clients need a great deal of time to develop the sense of safety and the necessary trust in the therapist before being willing to risk attending to anything new. They may need more time to develop the necessary contact with the therapist and even more time to tolerate the necessary contact with and trust in themselves. With these clients, the Gestalt therapist is present as an authentic self, responding with the support, validation, and love essential for the client's maturation.

The traditional hot-seat style of work is characterized by the therapist who assumes the role of mirror or of director of a drama in the client's life. This is an authentic and fruitful style for material that needs to be lifted out of confusion for clarity and affirmation. Another equally fruitful style is dialogic (Polster and Polster, 1973: Hycner, 1987), with the therapist present and available personally to focus on contact issues and other important material as a matter between the therapist and client, rather than the client and him- or herself exclusively. These approaches to the therapeutic situation will be explored fully and illustrated in chapter 6. The appendices consist of transcripts of two therapy sessions that illustrate these two styles.

Stages in the Course of Therapy

Since we are delineating an on-going Gestalt therapy process, we must note that the course of Gestalt therapy, as of any therapy, follows three, perhaps four, general stages. Many texts in counseling theory and practice delineate such stages (Egan, 1986). These stages include establishing a relationship, exploring a problem in depth, determining steps for the client to take, and providing support and encouragement for growth.

In the first stage, therapist and client must establish a working relationship, and the therapist must discover what "problems" the client came to explore, as well as ascertain the client's level of understanding and awareness, and the extent of the fear related to change. This stage may take anywhere from a few minutes to many months, depending on the amount of support that must be developed and the issues that emerge. The client's willingness or timidity, understanding or confusion, skill or naivete are the determining factors in the timing of this stage. Any client's resistance signals the limit of willingness, understanding, or skill and must be respected as well as confronted appropriately. The therapist's natural style must be flexible so far as language, timing, amount, and kind of contact are concerned. Often, the Gestalt therapist offers primarily supportive, reactive responses with some appropriate self-disclosures to promote the sense of security the client must have to proceed into the more difficult areas of experience. The primary tool in this stage is the clear, focused, but not demanding attention of the therapist.

In the second stage, the focus shifts to in-depth exploration. The client and therapist have developed a mutually agreeable contract as to the targeted phenomenon and work in tandem to achieve clarities and closures on the unfinished business that has surfaced, or on the apparent barriers to contact. What have been called "Gestalt techniques" were developed in the process of such exploration and experimentation as therapists creatively addressed the needs for clarity and contact.

Stage 3 in the course of therapy includes finding an answer to the question of what to do about the learnings that have been discovered

in Stage 2. In working with blocks to contact, some designated practices may be assigned as a kind of homework. Often, the blocks have
been habitual, and action to change habitual patterns is necessary; often
the psychological or spiritual awarenesses signal closure of the therapeutic course.

The fourth stage, if it is appropriate and necessary, consists in support of and feedback for the efforts to live with the new ideas, awarenesses, and behaviors that have emerged in therapy. The therapist
functions as a reinforcer of efforts and change, providing the client
with a sounding board related to the changing dimensions of the client's
life. Other client-therapist interactions are necessary to bring the relationship to an end.

Although many sessions are typically needed to reach the fourth
stage, all four stages may occur in one therapy session with a client.
With another client, the course of therapy may span several years.
Usually, the time needed for a successful therapy falls somewhere between these two extremes. Internal growth and change do not follow
a rational pattern and they unfold over varying amounts of time.
Sometimes the course of therapy follows an intermittent pattern: figural material is clarified and completed and after an interval other
material emerges.

All clients will not follow these stages in the exact order presented.
Clients are unique and present themselves uniquely. A therapist must
begin where the client is when he or she presents him/herself and proceed as the client is willing and able to work effectively through the
material presented. A Gestalt therapist uses clinical judgment in choosing the kinds of and the timing of interventions, accepting the fact that
some issues and dynamics may surface over and over again before
complete closure is reached.

How to Prevent Change

There are two primary ways we may prevent ourselves from growing and changing. They are polar opposites, as we shall see. One way
is to attempt to improve ourselves, to try to change. A person decides
that it is necessary to be "better" in some ways, and actively engages
in reading the right books, in physical exercise, or going on a diet.
People devote their energies to trying first one thing and then another
in order to achieve some imagined state they label as "better" or "im-
proved." As F. Perls says, "Many people dedicate their lives to actualize a concept of what they should be like, rather than to actualize
themselves . . . . This is again the curse of the ideal. The curse that
you should not be what you are" (1969, p. 19). The additional trap in

the self-improvement game is that most people are not only dissatisfied with what they are, they are also continuously searching outside themselves for what to become and for the means to become it. They are also continuously involved in neurotic efforts to keep from exposing their imperfections.

Recall the neurotic psychodynamics we discussed as manipulations of the self: the top dog, perfection-oriented or punisher part of the person continually makes demands; the person continually tries to change or improve; the underdog continually sabotages these efforts. The expectations of the top dog, having been introjected by the individual, usually are not reality oriented. Likewise, the underdog's main weapon of rationalization creates its own reality by accepting the demands for perfection, believing that such a state will never be realized, and by finding reasons or excuses for failure. The top dog says, "You should stop smoking," and the underdog replies, "I know, but I've tried and I am too weak, and all my friends smoke, and I need cigarettes to settle my nerves, and . . . ." Both top dog and underdog assume that we should change. The rationalizations balance against the demands and bypass the central knowing and choosing experience.

The second way in which one may prevent oneself from growing and changing is to frighten oneself with catastrophic expectations of what may happen if one really allows the authentic self to emerge, if one really allows oneself to feel, to experience, or to act in the ways that will satisfy needs, express true feelings and thoughts, or to complete gestalten. Instead of rationalizing and keeping the person stuck with trying to change, the underdog engages in scare tactics that often immobilize the person. The underdog says, "If you really told your wife that you are too tired to visit her mother, she'd . . . ." or "If you really told your husband that you don't want to entertain . . . ." or "If you asked that person out, you'd probably be turned down . . ." or "If you'd really tell your parents how angry you are, they wouldn't love you anymore." Such scare tactics are highly successful with neurotic individuals who are "unable to find and maintain the proper balance between (ourselves) and the rest of the world" (F. Perls, 1973, p. 31).

For the neurotic, then, the present environment and inner demands are experienced as pressing too strongly to allow the individual to react authentically; the self-structure is not strong enough to maintain itself against the pressures and demands as perceived. Two neurotic responses are available, both of which prevent growth and change and encourage ill health: the person may engage in self-improvement or, contrariwise, may frighten himself or herself with catastrophic expectations of the future and remain almost immobilized.

RELATIONSHIPS WITH
OTHER THERAPIES

Psychoanalytic Therapies

Gestalt therapy shares some basic premises with psychoanalytic and neoanalytic approaches to therapy. One essential agreement is there is a healing process that may be employed effectively for each individual. A further basis for agreement is that the individual is a complex arrangement of dynamic relationships. Understanding the dynamics of personality, then, is important in order to understand the total person and to employ effective therapeutic measures. How these dynamics are treated may vary from therapist to therapist, but a recognition of basic dynamics, such as defense mechanisms, is common to various psychotherapies.

Basic psychoanalytic theory makes several assumptions about personality and therapeutic processes that Gestalt therapy shares. The initial assumption is that a person is able to overcome neurotic mechanisms through some form of self-knowledge. That is, in the company of a therapist, the individual may bring to awareness past experiences, present emotions, and future intentions in such a way as to overcome neurotic manifestations of personality characteristics.

F. Perls was trained as a psychoanalyst; influences from psychoanalysis are evident in his writing. While Freud and F. Perls shared some general perspectives, Freud provided a set of perspectives about human psychodynamics and therapeutic practices against which F. Perls avowedly sharpened his own perceptions and practices. He differed from Freud in significant ways, as Edward W. L. Smith has pointed out in his essay delineating the roots of Gestalt therapy (1976). Paramount differences had to do with F. Perls' holistic-organismic position, with his adoption of basic Gestalt psychological concepts and his use of polarization principles and homeostasis. In therapy, F. Perls radically departed from psychoanalysis through his insistence on experience (here-and-now awareness), rather than description or discussion (talking about), as the primary mechanism.

Neoanalytic therapies also share significant concepts and principles with Gestalt therapy. Foremost among neoanalysts in influence was C.G. Jung, who postulated an individuation process occurring throughout life. According to Jung (1938), as the various elements and tendencies of the individual are actualized, that is, as the individual realizes the potential of all aspects of the self, the individual becomes more developed, more complete. The self tends to approach the maximum possible differentiation and actualization; the individuation process is the means whereby this is attained. Underdeveloped parts of the individual readily become factors that drain energy from the more developed areas of personality, leading eventually to neurotic mechanisms (Hall and Lindzey, 1978). This concern with the limiting effects of underrealized portions of the self also characterizes much of Gestalt therapy. In the Gestalt system, unrealized aspects of self are "disowned" by the individual, and it is only through the appropriate "reowning" of these aspects that the individual is able to become fully functional.

The concept of psychic energy, as developed by Jung, also is important in Gestalt therapy. Jung considered psychic energy a biologically-based "life energy." Gestalt therapy, too, treats this construct of energy as part of the natural functioning of the organism, but does not relate the concept of energy systematically to the overall structure of personality. Instead, the treatment of energy is more functional, a means of relating the individual's investment in present, past, or future activity. In these terms, investment of energy in unfinished, incomplete experiences draw energy away from present functioning, thus inhibiting the ability of the individual to participate fully in present experiences. Investment of energy in denying aspects or characteristics of the self also drains energy from the ongoing actualization of the individual.

A third significant construct from Jung's analytic theory is that of polarity (Polster and Polster, 1973). While Jung sees polarities as aspects of the overt personality, having counterparts in the "shadow," the Gestalt therapy view is that both poles are balanced in the personality, although neither may be in conscious awareness. Any part of the self has a counterpart that is available for knowing and understanding. Thus, Gestalt therapy postulates that behind every good little girl is a bad little girl ready to break free, and for every negative emotion there also is a positive counterpart. Allowing expression of the unexpressed or unaccepted qualities within the individual is pervasive in the therapy process. Therapeutic techniques designed to bring into awareness the polarities of experience enable the individual to become more complete and spontaneous.

One of the most spectacular and effective of the Gestalt therapy techniques, wherein the individual acts out dialogues between opposing parts and or feelings, is related to psychodrama as developed by J.L. Moreno (1964). The psychodrama technique allows the individual to stage a reenactment of an important event or a symbolic enactment of personal feelings or conflicts. In a group therapy setting, members of the group may take assigned parts, representing significant individuals so that persons may gain appropriate release of blocked emotions or awareness of personal dynamics contributing to problems in life. By providing a method of bringing the past into the present and acting out rather than discussing problems, psychodrama contributes much to contemporary therapeutic technique. The value of such role playing lies in the immediacy of the enactment, which transcends elaborate attempts at explaining or justifying behavior. While the Gestalt approach concentrates primarily on internal conflict and personal projections by having the client assume all of the roles that typically are distributed among members of a psychodrama group, the essential process of bringing experience into the here and now is the same.

From Wilhelm Reich, Gestalt therapy adopts the concept of muscular armor (Polster and Polster, 1973), wherein the individual is considered to lodge emotional responses in the body's musculature. Unacceptable emotions are repressed through habitual bodily mechanisms, many of which may consist of selectively tightening and restricting a particular muscle group. In Reichian therapy (1949), the actual relaxation of those rigidly protective armors is essential for releasing the individual's restricted energy. Gestalt therapy is an integrative act that pertains not only to the psychological world of the individual, but to the somatic world as well. Most recognizable of the influences from Reichian therapy is the attention to what the individual is doing physically at the moment, and focusing attention on the external behavior as an indication of what is occurring internally. Thus, the sensing body becomes a useful route to psychological awareness in Gestalt therapy.

The psychoanalytic theoretical postulations have been broadened and deepened by a focus on concepts of the self. These extrapolations of psychoanalytic theory derived from analysts interested in developing more cogent theory and more effective therapy for clients diagnosed as narcissistic or borderline in their personality character (Guntrip, 1969; Kohut, 1971, 1985; Masterson, 1985). Two theoretical strands, self-psychology and object relations psychology, have affected psychoanalytic schemata profoundly. Gestalt therapists and theorists have also evolved more clear conceptions of the self (Tobin, 1982; Yontef, 1983). Therapeutic interactions are better understood within Gestalt therapy theory because of this increased attention to the role of the self.

Cognitive Therapies

Cognitive therapies are constructed on the assumption that individuals' interpretations of themselves and their environment rule their behavior. The early writings and formulations of Alfred Korzybski (1933) apparently were influential in building a recognition in F. Perls and other Gestalt therapists that certain linguistic habits lead to misapprehension of reality. For example, the Gestalt emphasis on "I" language and changes in verbal expressions (e.g. "I have to . . ." changing to "I choose to . . .") owe much to Korzybski's General Semantics in which he claims that people are "unsane" to the extent that they use language to avoid direct perception of reality by constructing ever more abstract levels of interpretation. To recognize the world without providing labels and interpretations is to be "sane" in general semantics terms, as in Gestalt therapy recognition of the "obvious," the noninterpreted event, is a sign of healthy functioning.

Rational-emotive therapy (Ellis, 1958), likewise, shares orientations with early General Semantics formulations, particularly in the assumption that it is not events that cause people's unhappiness but their interpretations of events. Although Gestalt therapy is similar to rational-emotive therapy in this respect, the emphasis placed on personal symbolizing and blockage of experiences or the expressions of experiences differs from Ellis's emphasis upon ridding the individual of irrational assumptions and beliefs. Both therapies attempt to enable the client to explore nonfunctional beliefs with the goal of overcoming them in daily life. Gestalt therapy's orientation toward replacing intellectualizations with more direct and spontaneous feeling, true to the individual's personal experience, makes it less prescriptive than RET, which is directed toward teaching the client to think in certain rational ways.

Another cognitive therapy control theory (Glasser, 1985) emphasizes that the individual chooses total behaviors composed of actions, thoughts, emotions, and physiological responses, at any one moment. This choice means that the individual actually is much more in control of all aspects of life than is commonly believed. Glasser's insistence on the control each person has over his or her life is similar to the Gestalt therapy orientation that the individual chooses and controls, rather than being controlled by events or by others. It appears that control theory makes a stronger claim about the individual's control over all areas of life than does Gestalt therapy.

Existential and Phenomenological Therapies

Human existence is characterized by existential therapies by "being in the world"; the German word, *Dasein*, expresses the immediacy of personal experience as inseparable from the world. For the therapist to function effectively, awareness must be focused upon the immediate experiences and choices of the client, leading to an understanding of the client's own reality. Current experiencing is more salient for therapeutic interactions than the client's statements of problems from the past. Since the client has a unique world view and unique ways of understanding experiences, the therapist concentrates on those unique and specific nonintellectual processes by which the client experiences the world.

The existential therapy of Binswanger and Boss is oriented toward the whole person, eschewing dissection of the individual in favor of understanding the person in whole terms (Hall and Lindzey, 1978). Likewise, in Gestalt therapy, the client's on-going current experience is the basis for all awareness. The focus of the therapy is in the whole of the client's experience, the therapist's experience, and the interaction between the two. In fact, in the early development of Gestalt therapy, serious consideration was given to naming it "Existential therapy" (Rosenfeld, 1982). Writers in Gestalt therapy typically express the continuing interaction between therapist and client, as well as the intrapsychic world of the client, in existential terms, thus sharing intimately the world-view of existential therapies. In a closely related vein, Buber's (1958) formulation of the I-Thou relationship has been absorbed into Gestalt therapy as a cornerstone of the therapeutic relationship.

Phenomenological therapies, such as client-centered therapy (Rogers, 1951), are like Gestalt therapy in that they also concentrate on the world as experienced by the client. The basic assumptions of healthy self-regulation and the capacity to achieve full-functioning or self-actualization overlap with the Gestalt approach that recognizes the organismic wisdom of the individual. In fact, many Gestalt therapists use the vocabulary and constructs of phenomenology and existentialism in their work with clients because these ways of understanding the client's organismic functioning and the client-therapist relationship are consistent with the Gestalt concern with immediate functioning. In addition, the positive, optimistic viewpoint of client-centered therapy, which assumes that the individual's movement toward healthy adjustment includes adoption or retention of socially constructive attitudes and behaviors, is generally parallel with the Gestalt therapy assumptions of individual's relationships with others.

Behavior Therapies

The Gestalt approach places much emphasis on and is described as a phenomenological and existential approach to an understanding of people. Even though some of the basic assumptions differ, in its concentration upon a person's behavior and in dealing with the obvious, Gestalt therapy shares several major points of view with behavioral therapy. Both Gestalt and behavioral therapies state that we must deal with present behavior, that concentration on the past rarely leads to change, and that concern over the underlying reasons for behavior has limited therapeutic value. Both approaches begin by describing what persons are doing as opposed to what persons should do or have done.

In the behavioral approach, change occurs through shaping behavior by reinforcement, and the control of behavior is seen as primarily outside the person. The Gestalt approach accepts the existence of external reinforcers, but describes change as being initiated by choice based on internal awareness and beliefs rather than external controlling variables. The Gestaltist assumes that through awareness of internal processes the individual has a choice of behaviors. The behavioral therapist assumes that primary relationships among stimuli, behavior, and reinforcement are the most important, and awareness in itself does not necessarily lead to change.

Behavior therapies apply techniques derived from respondent (classical) conditioning and operant conditioning experiments to the immediate problems revealed by the client. Gestalt therapy, while it may share certain principles about the importance of current behavior, does not typically incorporate behavior therapy techniques.

SUMMARY

We have seen that, according to Gestalt therapists, growth and change are common to the human condition, and that persons are considered to have within themselves all of the ingredients and tools for living in healthy, satisfying, immediate interaction with their environments. Ill health results when such healthy possibilities are blocked, interrupted, or interfered with. Change processes are always present, and therapeutic change processes are those that confront the blocks and interruptions, and that bring clients to immediate awareness of what is being done, said, thought, or felt—statements of truth about the process of what the client is doing, feeling, thinking, or perceiving. These are two primary approaches that Gestalt therapists may take in therapeutic encounter as clients proceed through the stages in a successful therapy. There also are two ways in which change is prevented—by trying to change or to become what one is not by catastrophizing all of the risks related to potential change.

As clients mature, that is, move from dependence on environmental support to self-support, interventional strategies must change. The five steps in maturation are: (1) focus on present behaviors, overt or covert; (2) focus on old business, old traumas; (3) focus on a core self-concept; (4) focus on life decision making; and (5) focus on new behaviors. Clients move through these steps in unique ways with unique timing mechanisms and unique personal issues in each step. In the process of maturation, closure of unfinished gestalten is essential; impasses occur fre-

quently as limits of the experiences that are known and safe are reached
and new possibilities are experienced as frightening.

The total therapeutic process involves four stages: an introductory
stage for building trust and focusing on the present problem; a stage
for in-depth exploration; a stage in which the focus shifts to how to
use the learnings obtained; and a stage in which the therapeutic relationship is closed.

Gestalt therapy contains elements of theoretical and philosophical
positions found in other psychologies and therapies. It incorporates the
figure-ground perceptual principles of Gestalt psychology and defines
motivation in terms of the psychological need to complete gestalten.
There is some similarity to social learning theory in that people are
considered to learn as they continuously interact with all parts of their
environment. In this interaction, the symbolizing capability and self-
regulatory processes of individuals are of central psychological importance. Eastern psychological premises of holism and Jung's individuation process are also related, as are the acting-experiencing of psychodrama and the immediacy of obvious behaviors that are the focus in
behavioral therapies.

Chapter 5
Therapeutic Interventions

All therapists carry with them explicit and implicit standards regarding their clients. Such role expectations are derived from the experience and practice of therapists throughout the last century, regardless of their theoretical orientation, and from the formal theory of health, adjustment, and change espoused by the particular therapies themselves. Thus, while there may be some significant technical or theoretical differences among therapies, they share many common concerns and expectations. In fact, a famous study of Fiedler (1950) indicates that experienced therapists of whatever original, theoretical orientation share more concepts of appropriate therapeutic relationships with each other than do experienced and inexperienced therapists of the same theoretical orientation. This finding has led many therapists and researchers to conclude that the quality of the therapeutic relationship is of more lasting importance than the particular framework or orientation in which the therapist is trained.

While the centrality of the therapeutic relationship is unquestioned, Gestalt therapy is sufficiently different from other approaches to warrant a close look at modes and strategies. The foundation for interventions in Gestalt therapy lies in this dictum: the most potent interventions are existential, experiential, and experimental. The existential dimension leads the therapist to the here-and-now of interactions with clients; the experiential dimension focuses on the knowledge that emerges from awareness of any phenomenon; experimentation builds upon the belief that we learn the most important personal truths by discovering them for ourselves. We understand therapy to be "healing through meeting."

The three dimensions of existence, experience, and experiment are not arbitrary; they derive from the whole of Gestalt therapy, theory, and practice. Therefore, let us review three of the beliefs and assumptions upon which such therapeutic tools are based.

Recall the assumption of wholeness that is central in Gestalt therapy. Each person is a whole organism, whether or not that wholeness or aliveness is experienced. Personal experiences, of which the client may be unaware, are signaled in every aspect of the person—bodily feelings and movements, voices, tone, words, postures, images, and even dreams. The Gestalt therapist, in designing experiments to suggest to a client, may choose an intervention that focuses on any observed aspects of the encounter with the client. What is figural for the therapist may be a foot moving, a quality in the sound of the voice, the breathing process, or a pattern in verbal expression. As the client speaks, the therapist may become aware that an image is forming, based on what the client says, and may suggest using such images for therapeutic experimentation. There is wide latitude in the kind of observations that may trigger suggestions for experimentation.

Remember the phenomenological base in Gestalt therapy; each person construes the world uniquely, each is the sole arbiter of the world in which he or she lives. How the world is construed is described by Merleau-Ponty (1964), that is, there are levels of experience. The primary reality is the perceived life-world, the world constituted by the immediate, concrete, subjective experiences of the unique individual. It is the world of familiar, natural environmental components—both objects and persons. That world is one level of reality or experience. Other levels—activities of the mind—are of the imaginary, ideality, language, culture, and history (Edie, 1964). In Gestalt terms, the primary level is the immediacy of perception, sensory data, bodily experiences, and feelings. These data are triggers for mental activity and together are constituted into an experience of a life-world by the person's unique conscious awareness. Thus, the Gestalt therapist's focus is on experience, on the phenomena of the present—the experience of the client, the therapist's own experience, and the experience of the relationship.

Our considerations of psychodynamics are important here, particularly polarization. The individual establishes either-or categories or classifications that provide simple structures for reducing the complex relativistic phenomena encountered daily to discrete, predictable elements. A daughter either loves or hates her parents; a book that has been read has provided either a significant or an insignificant experience. The Gestalt therapist assumes the existence of such polarities. If a client reports experiences of deep depression, the therapist assumes the possibility of, or perhaps an earlier experience of, great joy. The therapeutic work often consists of experiments through which both poles of the client's experience are brought into awareness and affirmed, thus releasing the client to an ongoing perceptual, thinking, feeling, organismic flow of experience or to the choice of actions and behaviors that seem appropriate. Both poles of any inner experience are affirmed, as is the client's right to choose responses in any situation brought to the therapeutic encounter.

Finally, we believe that each person is motivated toward health, wholeness, and aliveness. The therapist does not attempt to pour life into the client; the therapist focuses on the mechanisms used by the client to block life from flowing freely through the body, mind, emotions, and behaviors. When life flows freely, there is also love, healing, and spiritual regeneration. Polster and Polster (Hycner, 1987) use the metaphor of light in describing the efficacy of therapy: "personal radiance" is released and expanded into action with "a sense of mutuality, and safety, and full function." The Gestalt therapist values the qualities of aliveness and radiance in each client, as well as the mechanisms used to block those qualities.

INTERVENTIONAL MODES
AND METHODS

Gestalt therapy is based on a person-in-environment model of living; in this model there are two foci: the individual person and the person-environment interaction. These foci are thus intrapersonal and interpersonal. The Gestalt therapist may choose either of these foci when working with clients. To translate them into interventional modes, the Gestalt therapist functions as a participant and an observer with a client. The therapist thus has two general modes of functioning: primarily as participant or primarily as observer. The most widely known mode, the observer, is exemplified in most of Fritz Perls' work where he served as a focused, clear, challenging observer or reflector. The focus is on the intrapersonal world of the client. The therapist's world is set aside so that it will not contaminate the client's in-depth exploratory processes. Krause (1977) describes this as "emptying myself" in order to be the therapist. The therapist then enters into a direct relationship with the world of the client, while the therapist's life experience forms the background of the therapeutic encounter; the immediacy of the client's contact with his or her world forms the figure.

The primarily participatory mode is described, in the writings of Polster and Polster, as being a dialogue between the therapist and client (Hycner, 1987). Since the kind of contact required for healthy functioning may be interpersonal as well as intrapersonal, the therapist becomes the presence with whom the client demonstrates good or poor environmental contact. In the participatory mode, the focus remains on the client and the immediacy of interaction. As opposed to the observer mode, in the participatory mode the therapist is more personally present; feels free to share some personal thoughts, feelings, or experiences; and uses the emerging material to explore the client's contact boundary processes. The blocks to good interpersonal contact may be neurotic coping patterns learned in early years (see chapter 3); these patterns are the target for intrapersonal work. In a sense, both modes involve significant dialogue. In the observer mode, the dialogue is primarily intrapersonal; in what we are calling the participatory mode, the dialogue is primarily interpersonal.

The therapist is both participant and observer in each mode, the difference being the amount and kind of personal involvement that seems appropriate in the immediacy of the therapeutic interaction. Both modes are I-Thou transactions in that the gestalt in each case includes the richness of the contact between the elements of the interaction. An I meets a Thou with the resulting reverberations in both persons that are inspirational, intimate, and spiritual. The therapist grows and changes as the client grows and changes.

There is no inherently right or wrong stance for the Gestalt therapist. In training and supervised work, therapists discover their personal or interpersonal focus: a top dog-underdog stalemate and a block the observer mode; some prefer to interact more directly with clients; some find that both are possible and use the mode that seems appropriate for clients. Often, in early stages of therapy, the interactive role is appropriate because the necessary trust is established as the client gets to know the person of the therapist. A classic confrontative encounter is not appropriate for clients who have minimal self-support or who lack a cohesive sense of self (Rosenfeld, 1982; Tobin, 1982). Clients who are naive in psychological exploration may be threatened by a therapist's stance as an observer and never allow themselves to explore the material that blocks them from healthy functioning. Interactive modes may be more appropriate. As Fagan (1970) pointed out, clients may need to learn how to be clients.

Two methods of structuring interactions with clients are available. In one method the material that emerges seems to suggest an intrapersonal or interpersonal focus: a top dog-underdog stalemate and a block in the contact with a significant person are examples of such a focus. The interventional method, in such cases, is based on a need to complete an unfinished gestalt. The alternate method is the method of choice when no clear focus emerges. In this case, the therapist follows as the client relates the figural material, whatever it is, and simply makes suggestions that facilitate clarification in the on-going encounter. The unfinished gestalten being focused on are of a different kind and level of experience, usually less deeply seated and of shorter duration. An underlying dimension of experience emerges as the client and the therapist stay in contact with each other and current in their interaction.

COMPLETION OF GESTALTEN

The goals of therapy are twofold: awareness and acknowledgment of personal experience regardless of content and, issuing from that, the activation of the self-support system of the client through conscious and responsible choices, thereby facilitating good contact. The first goal, awareness and acknowledgment of personal experience, is the central ingredient in the completion of gestalten that heretofore have been incomplete. Awareness of what has been repressed or avoided may lead to the sense of closure for which the organism is striving.

The Gestalt therapist believes that closure comes with the experience of "personal congruence" (Rogers, 1959; Gendlin, 1962). Carl Rogers defines personal congruence as the state in which "the self as perceived equals the actual experience of the organism, accurately symbolized" (1959, p. 206). In this statement, we note three parts of the congruent experience: the self as perceived, the actual experience of the organism, and the accurate symbolization of the actual experience. When all three are equal, congruence is experienced.

A female client says, "I am really okay. I don't know why I am here," while her hands are clenching and unclenching. She may become aware of the clenching, aware of feelings of frustration associated with the clenching, and she says, "I am really frustrated about my job." With just the right intonation and intensity, she acknowledges that the whole of her experience is a part of her self-structure. At that moment, she experiences congruence; the "felt meaning" is experienced as truly represented in the words being spoken (Gendlin, 1967). The personal meaning, beyond the mere words employed, is affirmed with a sense of inner relief. At that moment, the gestalt regarding the client's frustration is completed, a previously disowned or unaware aspect of herself is integrated, and she is free to fully experience whatever her organism brings to her awareness in the next moment.

In the context of on-going therapy, much unfinished business may be uncovered; the need to reach closure on gestalten may surface many times. In each case, closure of gestalten involves four steps: expression, differentiation, affirmation, and choice/integration. We shall look at each of these in turn.

Expression

The first step in any therapy, including Gestalt therapy, is to express overtly, in some fashion, what the inner experience is so that it can be looked at objectively. In our earlier discussions, we considered some aspects of the assumption that each person is a dynamic whole, even though the psychological experience may be of fragmentation. We considered that each person, being whole, would portray personal experience in every aspect of being—words, tone of voice, images, and body movements. These aspects will signal the person's inner experience in some way. The therapist will observe such signals as a tapping foot, a harsh tightness in voice quality, or shallow breathing, and will facilitate the client's awareness of these overt manifestations of possible distress. The therapist suggests and the client either knows the meaning or can discover the meaning of his or her experience.

For example, a male client recounts an incident that happened with his wife. As he talks, his voice is fairly steady, his posture is erect, his feet are crossed, and his hands rest on the arm of his chair. He relates the incident slowly and at one point, although nothing in his voice or posture changes, his right foot moves up and down in a fashion discrepant with the rest of his self-presentation. His foot is signaling some inner process that is not being considered overtly. The therapist may decide to suggest some experimentation that can bring out the foot signaling, and the client may agree to take a look at whatever inner phenomenon the active foot signals. Only when the inner experience is brought out overtly can therapeutic interaction take place.

Differentiation

The second stage in the therapeutic process is differentiation. Because the roots of conflict, confusion, depression, or anxiety lie in the processes used to prevent the client from full and complete experience, one of the assumptions that can be made is that an inner battle is probably going on. The male client may have some kind of battle between the aspect of himself that recounts the "problem" and the aspect represented in his foot motion. He releases conflicting sides by differentiating between them. Through awareness, the processes in which one is engaged are experienced and recognized. The interaction between conflicting parts is the most important thing to recognize, but it remains hidden unless the conflicting factions or aspects are separated.

The goal of the differentiation stage is to facilitate the client's recognition of the alienated, disowned, or fragmented selves within. The therapist's primary tool is experimentation: suggesting activities through which the client may clarify the confused aspects of the inner experience. In the case of the male client described above, the therapist may suggest personalizing the energy that keeps his foot moving. The therapist may simply call attention to the foot motion and suggest that the client move the foot faster or more intensely—exaggerate the motion. The therapist may suggest that the foot could be seen as having a life and voice of its own. At this stage, interventions are intended to concretize the client's experiences and to facilitate awareness of them. Interventions come from the creative therapist's own awarenesses, learnings, thoughts, and ideas. Zinker ((1977) notes the following characteristics of the creative therapist:

- a good sense of timing;
- the capacity to detect where the person can be reached, energized, moved emotionally;
- a knowledge of where the psychological "buttons" are and when to push them;
- the ability to shift gears—to let go of some things and move on to other, more lively areas;
- the willingness to push, confront, cajole, persuade, energize the person to get the work done;
- and the wisdom to know when to let the person stay confused so that he or she may learn to develop his or her own clarity. (pp. 57–58)

Our male client may become aware that in his foot movement he is expressing his frustration with his relationship with his wife or her actions, which was not being expressed in his voice, words, or other body movements. The frustration probably has been suppressed; his allowing it to surface only in his foot and without conscious awareness would indicate that it has been given little attention. By becoming aware of his frustration, he has the opportunity to differentiate it from the thoughts or behaviors that are manifest in his words and tone.

Affirmation

This next stage follows differentiation immediately: the therapist encourages the client to affirm the various differentiated parts. Some therapists use the term "acceptance" here: the client is encouraged to accept all of the parts that are emerging into awareness. Some therapists use the term "affirmation" or "identification with." At this stage, clients are encouraged to invest themselves in their experiences, and to acknowledge or affirm them, even if they do not necessarily like what is emerging. "I am my foot; I am frustrated," and "I am my voice,

and I am controlling myself in order to prevent my parents from knowing that I am having marital problems," for example. Both statements
may be true, even though conflicting.

A friend of ours recounts a time in her life in which she was going
through a number of changes and was uncertain about her goals. In
order to keep focused on how she felt at any one time and to convince
herself that it was all right with her to be in flux, she devised a verbal
formula. In it she would make a statement about what she was aware
of doing—even the most simple tasks or the most awful feelings—and
then say, "and that's okay." She did not always feel okay, but the
simple verbal acknowledgment continually discriminated the okay part
from the not-okay part and encouraged an affirmation that, no matter
what the content of the awareness, she was truly doing it. This general
acknowledgment of herself was the start toward determining what she
really wanted and toward the clarity and strength to choose for herself.

An important inhibitor of acceptance or acknowledgment of oneself
is the belief that a person must always be consistent. The need for
consistency, however, is often closely tied to the demand for perfection. In reality, each person can and does contain contradictions, par-
adoxes, and inconsistencies. Complexity and changeability may be central ingredients in the gestalt formation and completion processes.

With the acknowledgment of inner conflicting or warring elements,
the client may see a life pattern emerging that had been hidden in the
confusion or in the problem being managed. Our male client may become aware that he has spent most of his life pretending to his parents
that his life is progressing smoothly in order to keep a good image with
them or to keep their love and attention. Such life patterns are common. Or, he may discover that he is also controlling himself so that his
wife will maintain a good image of him. He may discover a 6-year-old
child within himself, who never felt accepted. Any of a myriad of other
patterns might emerge from the seemingly simple experiment of moving his foot and becoming aware of its meaning for him.

One further aspect of the affirmation stage is very important. With
awareness and affirmation of the experimental phenomenon also comes
the awareness and affirmation of the individual's responsibility for those
phenomena. Our male client may say, "I am my foot, I am frustrated.
And I am responsible for my frustration. I am not responsible for my
wife's behavior that triggered it. I am responsible for my own reactions
to her behavior." Or he may say, "I am responsible for living my life
in order to gain my parents' approval. I am not responsible for them
and their demands on me. I am responsible for my perception of their
demands and for what I have done and am doing in response to their
demands, as I perceived them." As F. Perls says, "Responsibility is

really response-ability, the ability to choose one's reactions" (1973, p. 79). Part of the work of the therapist is to help clients to be clear regarding the aspects of their experiences for which they are willing to take responsibility, and to be aware of where the limits of personal responsibility are set.

Accommodation and Choice

The completion of gestalten through affirmation of personal awareness and responsibilities brings a new stage in therapy with two new psychological necessities: accommodation and choice. When the client becomes clear about differing parts and owns them, the client is free to choose behaviors that fit either one or both in a time of accommodation and choice. "It is at this stage where behavior may be awkward and poorly coordinated, and the patient feels clumsy . . . the world is not as obliging as one might like . . . the patient [must] move past exclusive focus on him/herself . . . to pay close attention to the effect that his or her words and actions have on others (M. Polster, 1987, p. 321)." The client we have been describing is free to choose his behavior with his wife. He may choose to confront his wife with his frustration, he may choose to be honest with his parents concerning his conflicting feelings, or he may make any of several other possible choices. Made with awareness and affirmation, any of these choices may be right for the client at that time.

The client's "problem" may be resolved through the choices made. The goal for the therapist, however, is the educated awareness of the client as to what he or she is doing, how it is being done, and any life patterns that may emerge from these awarenesses. Awareness and conscious acknowledgment facilitates choice by enabling the individual to be what he or she is, without trying to be what he or she is not.

In the first transcribed therapy session (Appendix A), the stages in the therapeutic process and the sense of calmness and satisfaction at closure, at least for that session, are noted.

INTERVENTIONAL STRATEGIES

Therapy is primarily an art form. While many who have viewed films of Fritz Perls' workshop therapy see those demonstrations as the work of an artist and have gained insight into some particulars of Gestalt technique, on-going, long-term therapy does not follow the patterns of Perls' demonstrations. In on-going therapy, the Gestalt therapist must balance clinical assessments of a client's strengths and weaknesses, the client's stage in the maturational process, and the client's perceived limits with the therapist's clinical and artistic armamentarium (Hycner, 1987). The Gestalt therapist is an artist as well as a clinician. Given the rich mix of possibilities in the client's presentation of self at whatever stage of the maturational process; given the open endedness of the therapist's existential, experiential, and experimental stance, the choices of interventional strategies to use at any point are multifarious.

The attitude of respect—Polster and Polster (Hycner, 1987) call it reverence—for the personhood of the client indicates the only limit so far as the therapist is concerned. Therapy starts with the client's presentation and proceeds with suggestions based on the assessment of what the client is willing and able to comprehend, to tolerate emotionally, or to incorporate into his or her self-structure. What is done depends on how the I-boundary functions and how permeable the core constructs are. A balance must be maintained between the need for safety and security and the suggestions for experimentation, which may be emotionally risky.

Flexibility is the key element in the choice of strategy for any therapeutic situation. Gestalt therapy literature contains several presentations of "games," "rules," and specific techniques (Greenwald, 1972; Hatcher and Himelstein, 1976; Levitsky and F. Perls, 1970; Yontef, 1971). However, when a therapist depends on techniques as working tools, the coherence of the Gestalt approach will be missed. The therapist who is bound by a set of techniques has little choice in the therapeutic situation; the design of the technique controls the encounter instead of awareness of the client's experience as the operative factor. A therapist who follows a set of techniques is functioning in a closed system (ideas and thoughts) as opposed to an open system (organismic responses). For example, it is known that in many persons there is a pattern that relates guilt, resentment, demands, forgiveness, and gratefulness. The therapist may direct a client to express guilt as resentment, turn resentment into explicit demands, and then encourage expression of whatever forgiveness and gratefulness are experienced. However, this pattern and movement from one to another emotion is not always present. A client may affirm guilt feelings and experience closure at that point, so far as the immediate work is concerned. In pushing the client to complete the pattern by proceeding to resentment and demands, the therapist is relying upon a set formula. The therapist who functions in an open system knows the formulas and is willing to abandon any structures in favor of observations of the moment-to-moment signals the client is giving about the on-going experience. Creative experimentation is called for. This is the sense in which Gestalt therapy is an art form.

Sometimes the client will present clearly defined experiences for experimentation. More often, however, the client is experimenting with new and heretofore unsuspected material. An impasse occurs because the experience is fraught with risks related to leaving the known and moving out into the unknown. Psychologically, such movement requires that some self-support be present and that the client trust the therapist to an exceptional degree. The client may balk—express fear of the experiment being suggested or deflect and avoid dealing with something the therapist says or suggests. Then the shape of the client's fear becomes a psychological entity to be dealt with through experimentation.

Many therapists feel that the whole of a therapeutic interaction might be characterized as dealing with resistance. Some therapists confront resistance head-on; others deal with it more gently, letting the client move slowly and giving him or her no antagonist, no one to resist. Such therapeutic choices fall within the style and beliefs of the individual therapist.

One important set of therapeutic techniques that must be singled out for emphasis are those that deal with verbal communications. Often, a client may be threatened by an abrupt movement into imagery or body experience; such personal experiences may have been cut off from awareness since childhood. Verbal communication is often the primary representational device, and, although it is the most subject to distortion or confusion, it is the least threatening to a client. Bandler and Grinder (1975) have suggested that what has seemed like "magic" in the therapeutic work of F. Perls, Virginia Satir, Milton Erickson, and other "charismatic superstars" is in large part related to the way in which these therapists see through the structures of the language being used to the meta-level processes that underlie it. The client's pain, frustration, and confusion lie there. Such seeming "magical" therapeutic work can be understood by studying the linguistic bases of the language; learning the primary ways in which the language may distort, delete, or generalize the experience; and designing experiments through which the deep structure of the language may emerge so that underlying meanings and feelings may surface.

Another powerful therapeutic medium in Gestalt therapy is imagery or dreams. Both media involve the emergence of the contents of the preconscious, that part of the psychological experience that is not in the conscious awareness but is available to awareness. Imagery is active while the conscious rational thought processes are interrupted; dreams emerge while they are dormant. In Gestalt therapy, both dreams and images are considered to be avenues through which unfinished gestalten emerge into awareness. Although the symbolic "language" is metaphoric—that is, any image may mean anything and usually does signal meanings far removed from the nominal content—it is rich in therapeutic possibilities.

In choosing to intervene in one aspect of the client's experience, such as the imagery, the therapist keeps efficiency and effectiveness in mind. Immediacy experiences are simple rather then complex in idea, and deep rather than superficial in emotional content. Often, the therapist prefers to explore nonverbal rather than verbal avenues. The use of art materials in therapy is often advantageous. A sketch of an image, using crayons and drawing paper, may expedite awareness and lead to experiences of great depth and intensity. Interventions using body awareness may also be helpful in a client's work in difficult and threatening areas of experience. The client's awareness of and consent to what is being done is critical.

Since images, fantasies, or dreams are seen as metaphoric expressions of content of the self-experience, a therapist may use techniques that raise recessed material to a conscious level. The client's willingness to interrupt the conscious controls customarily placed on imagined material, or the willingness to interact with content from a dream that may seem bizarre or unusual, releases preconscious material into recognizable structures and patterns. The medium is bringing a message to the client.

First person experiences are the most powerful because they sustain direct contact with events being dealt with. Contact with disowned or disliked aspects of the self is difficult to maintain. Clients may say, "You know how you feel when you think about a bad experience," instead of what may really express the first person experience—"I feel very sad." Staying with the "I" of experience is rewarding and demanding, especially in dreams or imagery work in which the meta-level content may be intense and powerful. Each aspect of a dream may be seen as a projection of some facet of the client or the world he or she experiences.

Whether the therapeutic medium is body language, imagery, verbalization, or dream, an essential ingredient in therapy is what may be called "acting." The client is encouraged to allow him- or herself to be and to act for the attributes, actions, feelings, or persons involved in the polarities being focused upon. Naranjo (1976) points out that the acting out of polarities within the individual serves to implement expression by transferring experience from one expressive modality to another, that is, to give motoric expression to an idea or image. Thus, by avoiding the usual verbalizations as means of exploring personal experience, the individual heightens involvement in the therapy in a physical, nonverbal fashion.

Classic Experiments

Thus far, we have presented some generalizations about therapeutic techniques. In addition to these general principles, there are "classic experiments," techniques that have been used with good results; some of them have become a part of the general skills package. From our previous discussion, the techniques may now be seen as efforts to arrive at both clarity and the psychological closure state of owning or claiming what is clearly experienced.

Dialogue. This technique is known colloquially as the "empty chair" experiment, and it is probably the best known and most often adopted by therapists of other orientations. It is a primary tool for achieving clarity. Whatever aspect of the client's world is not clear is separated from the client psychologically by the device of imagining it in a chair or some other place where the client can address it. Giving voice to the thoughts and feelings of both the client and the unclear part in a dialogue can bring insight and clarity. Both poles of an experienced phenomenon can be explored.

Exaggeration. In dealing with confusion, particularly where feelings are involved, it is often appropriate for the therapist to suggest that the client exaggerate some motion or some speech pattern. Feelings that have not been dealt with may not surface clearly until such an experiment is tried. The client may not be aware of the truth of a statement until exaggeration brings the inner experience into focus.

Reversal. Polarities are always present, and the reversal technique usually brings out the existence of both poles. Hate and love may both be present; needs to reach out and to pull back often exist simultaneously. To suggest that a client reverse a statement as an experiment often is useful in awakening awareness of essential ingredients in effecting closure.

Rehearsal. In arriving at clarity from confusion, a client may need to try to cut out or rehearse different sentences. Sometimes a client becomes aware of the truth of personal experience only in the act of speech. At the impasse in therapeutic work, when the client has reached the limit of environmental support but the self-support system is not yet strong, he or she may have catastrophic expectations regarding any change. Explicitly stating these fears and expectations often helps in confronting the imagined catastrophies by adding a missing reality contact.

Making the Rounds. In working with a client to discover some personal truth, a therapist may suggest an experiment for a client to rehearse with each member of the group present at the time. Contact with individual group members brings a human environmental dimension that often helps the client to be clear.

Exposing the Obvious. F. Perls had one dictum for therapists: pay attention to the obvious. The deep structures and processes are often revealed in a client's first statements or obvious movements. Techniques to expose the obvious are usually reports of observations of what the client is doing. "Are you aware of any sensation in your jaw?" is an example of an observation a therapist might make when noticing some tightness in the client's jaw muscles.

Directed Awareness Experiments. Contact is an essential ingredient in the therapeutic process—contact with both the personal inner experience and the experience of the outside world. Clear seeing, hearing, and touching, as well as clear sensations in the body are the bases for contact. A therapist often designs experiments to enable a client to be aware of ways in which sensory data may either be contaminated or ignored.

Experiments with the I-Boundary

Classic experiments are those that have been known and used for some time. We have repeated them as previously limned because of their classic nature. However, in the 10 years since the previous edition was written, the importance of contact has been reaffirmed. It was a central piece in *Gestalt Therapy* (Perls et al., 1951) and was later downplayed when Fritz Perls' workshop therapy became the prevailing model for Gestalt therapy. Now, one issue remains for discussion in this section on techniques. The therapeutic work of the client is experiential and experience is centered in personal interactions at what the Polsters call the "I-boundary" (Polster and Polster, 1973). The I-boundary is made up of many points at which interaction is permitted, such as encounter with other persons, with thought processes (ideas, images, memories, and so forth), with actions, with values or beliefs, or with objects in the environment. In each engagement there are two aspects: the arousal of a primary experience of the outside world and resonance within the self that is stirred by the contact. The resonance includes a knowledge of whether the arousal initiates welcome experience or one that is too risky to contemplate or act upon. The I-boundary, then, represents the limit of what the person permits the self to encounter meaningfully. Contact is made outside the I-boundary and therefore is always immediate, always experimental, and always risky.

When a healthy person is engaging in permissible interactions (contacts), there is ease and excitement; the person is nourished and enlivened. In the neurotic person, permissible interactions may be controlled to the point of boredom or deadness. A therapist suggests experiments with a client in order to discover the limits to whatever psychological configuration is being explored. Laura Perls notes that "experience is on the boundary . . . . If you go too quickly beyond the boundary, you may feel unsupported, actually, that's what I work with: a concept and experience of contact *and* support. Certain supports are necessary and essential. Other supports are, well, desirable and possibly usable. The lack of essential support always results in anxiety" (Rosenfeld, 1982, p. 18).

There is no royal road to therapeutic change; there are probably as many avenues to successful therapy as there are therapists to choose them. Choices of interventions are matters of creativity, training, and experience. The art and skill of the Gestalt therapist are engaged in designing experiments or using classic ones that will move the client to the contact boundary, clarify the boundary functions (seeing, hearing, touching, feeling), and mobilize self-support for meaningful, clear, and authentic contacts that are both nourishing and exciting. Other important criteria are ease, efficiency, and effectiveness as well as personal preference. All of this must be accomplished while communicating radical respect for whatever the client presents.

Now that you have read the sections on steps and stages in the therapeutic process and on interventions in therapy, you may wish to turn to the appendices to study the transcripts of sessions illustrating their appearance as a therapist works with a client. Notes will be found on the stages of therapy and on the techniques and attitudes of the therapist.

INDIVIDUAL AND GROUP WORK

Two models for group/client/therapist interaction are noted in the Gestalt literature (Cohen, 1970; Derman, 1976; Zinker, 1977). Since the earlier edition of this work was published, the emphasis on group process has shifted, so that although the classic group model is still practiced, the dialogical small group (also called "group interactional") has become more popular (Frew, 1986) and is seen as a vehicle for experimenting with contact styles of participants. We will discuss each model in turn.

The classic model was developed and practiced by Fritz Perls and is used currently by many therapists who trained with or were influenced by him. In this model, the therapist is available for work with one person or one experiential phenomenon at a time. The volunteer client takes the "hot seat" facing the therapist, sometimes in the center of the group and sometimes in the circle of group members. While the therapist and client explore whatever phenomena emerge in their interaction, the rest of the group members remain silent and are spectators, not unlike the Greek choruses who replied to or commented on the dramatic action in the play. Although limited, the chorus performed an essential function, as does the group in Gestalt therapy. At certain points the group may be called into the action by the therapist, but usually this is done in a structured way to further the client's work. For example, the therapist may have the client "make the rounds"; that is, go to each member of the group with the same sentence or sentence fragment that emerged from the work. An example might be, "I want you to like me for my . . ." and the client then finishes the sentence with words that fit a "here-and-now" awareness of each person.

When the therapist allows it, the group members may reply briefly with their own reactions. The controlling factor in the client's interactions with the group members is the therapist's intention to keep the focus on the client and to encourage that person to take responsibility for his or her own experience, not to allow support for unhealthy behavior and not to allow other group members to intrude their own perceptions and values into the client's work. The therapist is the dominant force in the F. Perls model.

The client usually remains in the "hot seat" anywhere from 10 to 30 minutes, although a longer time may be involved; the work is terminated only when the client and therapist have some sense of closure or some clear statement from the client that he or she is finished. Typically, from two to four participants take the "hot seat" during any 2- to 3-hour group session.

The second model might be called the "group interactional" model. It has also been called the "Gestalt group process" (Zinker, 1977) or the "Gestalt thematic approach" (Derman, 1976). In this model, the therapist is the authority and director of experimentation; however, the therapist is more flexible and more attuned to and permissive of suggestions from other group members. Group interaction is legitimized and a group cohesiveness is allowed to emerge, even encouraged. The work of one client might awaken awareness of a common experiential theme, which might then be explored by an activity in which all group members could be involved.

Group activity might start when the work of one client elicits awareness of a lack of feeling in some part of the body. Other group members may express similar awarenesses, enough communality for the therapist to suggest that an imagery experiment in which all of the group members share may be appropriate. The data from this exercise will then possibly provide the content and material for an entire session, with several members working for closure on the awareness that emerged. Work can also trigger social awareness, commonalities, or the sense of community, which could be explored. In this model, the work of each group member has "social significance . . . dynamic value, a presence in the group. . . . The group becomes a microcosm of our actual social environment" (Zinker, 1977, pp. 163, 164).

In both models, Gestalt group therapy does not involve a prolonged relationship with a group while patients slowly reconstruct their original relationship(s) or analyze aspects of experience in which they learned to block or to disown aspects of the self. It is a short-term, intense, dramatic, supportive, and confrontative form of group therapy, usually lasting months rather than years. Each group member experiences himself or herself as a unique individual and a social group member.

Several comments may be found in Gestalt literature about the value of the group in therapy. Greenwald mentions the "atmosphere of safe risk taking . . . the attitude of open self-expression within the group that enables the participants to experience honest interaction between himself and others" (1972, p. 102). He also mentions "silent self-therapy" that occurs with group members when they are empathic witnesses to a genuine experience with which they may identify closely. Cohen reports that her students experienced "greatest personal involvement in spite of the fact that they were spectators rather than interacting most of the time . . . in the truest sense of identification and purification of a Greek drama" (1970, p. 138). Brown (1978) discusses another function of the group experience: "In some measure it provides for the participants what ritual activities do in primitive societies . . . evoking strong emotion, of distancing this emotion sufficiently to make it bearable, and of discharging the emotion, providing release and satisfaction" (p. 68).

SUMMARY

The centrality of the client/therapist relationship is unquestioned in Gestalt therapy. However, the quality of the interventions is different from many other approaches, being at once existential, experiential, and experimental. That is, the most powerful interventions are focused in the present, are awareness-oriented rather than discussed, and are based on the understanding that important personal learning is made through a discovery process. Two therapeutic modes are available to the therapist—primarily as participant or primarily as observer; both are valid I-Thou transactions. Choice of mode depends on needs and limitations of clients and personal stylistic preferences of therapists. Two methods are also available, depending on the client's presentation of material: a structured dramatic experience in which elements are available and the gestalt is unfinished, or a less structured method in which the focus is more limited and the gestalt emerges out of the smaller elements as they are classified. Gestalt completion requires four mechanisms: expression, differentiation, affirmation, and closure/integration.

Interventions in Gestalt therapy practice arise out of the experimental set of the therapist. There are some classic statements of "rules and games"; however, in the immediacy of the therapeutic encounter, the creativity of the therapist devises interventions in keeping with the client's willingness and ability to explore images, body movements, voice quality, eye contact, and verbalizations. The goal is to facilitate awareness, gestalt completion, and movement into the risky experience of the next emergent gestalt.

Interventional settings are both one-to-one, usually in a private office or other private settings and in group experiences. Groups may be structured as background for one-to-one work or as interactional arenas in which work emerges out of the interactions of group members. Interventional strategies are limited only by the I-boundary experiences of clients and by preferred modes and styles and experiences of therapists.

Chapter 6
The Therapist

As Isadore From (Brown et al., 1988) has stated, the central aspect of the Gestalt therapist's presentation of self is *integrity*—authenticity and humane beliefs. Without authenticity, the therapist's functions will either be diluted or destructive. Authentic presence must be based on the phenomenological orientation and the beliefs that Gestalt therapists hold in common.

The Gestalt therapist is an artist, creating each moment of a therapeutic relationship with an appropriate ambience and set of tools related to the client's needs. In this chapter, we provide a discussion of the therapist's personal qualities and functions with clients.

THE THERAPIST AS PERSON

Authenticity

The competent Gestalt therapist, a trained professional, has reached a high level of personal awareness and ability to maintain awareness of personal processes, including a sense of humor that can be very therapeutic for both client and therapist. This does not mean that the therapist always functions as a model human being, but it does mean that the therapist provides additional facilitation of growth and change in the client by being an appropriate model of the healthy processes promoted in Gestalt therapy. The therapist's own awareness, assimilated skills and knowledge of theory and dynamics, and his or her personal characteristics are integrated. The therapist is able to trust the organismic flow of experience during the therapy session, because the therapist is aware of and deals directly with needs and desires. Instead of denying intuitive private experience in favor of clinical analysis, the therapist integrates the two while working with the client. In short, the therapist is authentic, whole, and genuine, just as the client is encouraged to be (Bugenthal, 1965).

Authentic behavior in the therapist is important in several ways. When the therapist is authentic, the possibility of building trust with the client increases dramatically. Spontaneous, flowing responses to new situations on the part of the therapist heighten the interaction between therapist and client. The willingness to be authentically oneself and to express oneself fully in the role as therapist or group leader seems to be an effective approach, no matter what particular therapeutic approach is taken. For instance, Orlinsky and Howard (1967) report that good psychotherapeutic hours may be collectively described as experimental. They characterize these sessions as being highly symmetrical and collaborative sessions wherein both therapist and client experience a warm, emotionally expressive relationship with each other. Such experiential sessions occur only if the therapist is secure and integrated enough to be able to respond authentically and spontaneously to the evolving situation.

People respond positively and meaningfully to the authentic person, or at least to what they perceive as authenticity. Most people are constantly wary of phonies on all levels, from high government positions to intimate personal relationships. The authentic person is perceived as a trustworthy person—even in situations where strong disagreement prevails. While trust is important in daily interactions, it is essential in therapy. The client will explore and confront the meaning of personal experience only when there is a belief that the therapist is trustworthy. When therapists take responsibility for and express their anxiety, fear, fatigue, their need to show off, or their need to make a good impression, they will increase the possibilities of the session. Although one cannot guarantee that clients will respond favorably to these disclosures, one can be certain that, unless the therapist owns and expresses personal, meaningful experience, any trust or change is far less likely to occur.

Phenomenological Orientation

Gestalt therapy (as well as client-centered therapy, psychodrama, existential therapy, and logotherapy) takes a phenomenological stance with regard to the therapeutic relationship. That is, there is a belief that the therapist can work best with the client by entering into his or her phenomenological world, experiencing along with the client the client's perspectives. This orientation requires a close, personal relationship with the client. The therapist cannot be aloof, distant, or totally objective in interaction. The therapist, therefore, needs to be able to understand the client's personal feelings, beliefs, thoughts, and values in order to respond fully to those aspects of the client. The therapist must participate as well as observe.

From the phenomenological perspective, certain therapeutic goals (such as adjustment to the social environment), certain traditional therapeutic strategies (such as exploration of personal history and use of interpretation), and certain methods of focusing on change (such as logical or rational analysis of the situation) may be used but are not seen as central in the therapy process; they may, in fact, be counterproductive. Rogers (1951), for example, emphasizes that the therapist should communicate a sincere, unconditional acceptance of the client and the client's feelings. Gestalt therapy, too, is directed toward the client's personal experience of the world, and uses this experience as the starting point for further therapy.

The phenomenological perspective also leads the therapist toward concern with the immediate, current experience of the client. In fact, in Gestalt therapy, it is of paramount importance for the therapist to stay with the client's present experience and to facilitate his or her present awareness. It is through attention to the present, on-going flow of experience that unresolved personal conflicts emerge and become resolved. This cannot be achieved through a discussion of the past or of noncentral characteristics of the present.

One of the authors had the following experience, which illustrates the difference between exploring the current experience and the non-central or past experience. During a graduate training class in Gestalt therapy, the instructor assumed the client "role" in order to provide one of the students an opportunity to practice the Gestalt therapy strategies in working with dream material. To do this, the instructor, who did not have a current dream to explore, recalled a dream from the past with the intention of using it to create a practice therapy situation for the student. As the dream work began, the instructor very carefully told the details of the dream to the student, and began what should have been a true exploration of the current personal meaning of the dream. However, the therapist actually began to invent details to try to recreate old emotional responses to the dream, and to organize the dream so as to provide a good learning experience for the student. This involved much thinking and planning in order to make the experience seem "real." The student, however, quickly realized that the dream was being contrived, and, instead of merely following the program of the instructor, centered his attention on what the instructor actually was doing. That is, he asked the instructor to describe what was really occurring at that moment. With his reorientation away from the dream and toward the instructor's current experience, the "practice therapy session" became a real therapy session. It led into a meaningful session

regarding the instructor's desires to have everything in the environment carefully planned and controlled in advance. Thus, the current
experience of planning, organizing, and controlling, once it was explored in therapy, was revealed to be a salient area for personal awareness.

Many times, the client will attempt to fulfil what is assumed to be
the expectations of the therapist. When the client tries to alter personal
awareness or experience to coincide with the perceived goals of the
therapist, the client is playing the role of "good client." That role in
itself may be more important for the exploration of current experience
than the stated topic. The therapist, therefore, needs to be attuned to
the contrived as well as to the spontaneous moments in therapy and
to facilitate the honest exploration of present experience.

Belief System

Since clients present both neurotic coping mechanisms and negative
self-structures, the Gestalt therapist must necessarily maintain both artistic skill in focusing on the mechanisms and a radical respect for the
client. That radical respect is based on the unqualified belief that each
client who comes into therapy has within himself or herself the means
and methods for living in a personally satisfying way. It is an unalter-
able belief that health is available. Clients need to know that they are
not crazy, that they are not beyond repair, and that what they experience is understandable. The beliefs of the therapist are an essential
ingredient in the metamorphic process through which the client's self-
support system is uncovered and sustained.

Some clients sense the therapist's beliefs and do not need to confront them directly. Clients need a basis for developing a positive self-
image. A therapist's belief may be the essential ingredient in starting.
One client may need to be told repeatedly, over a long period of time,
that the presenting dynamics may be changed; another may pick up
the therapist's belief from the kinds of interactions that attend the therapeutic encounter.

One of the authors recalls the experience of having seen a young
man, a student, in weekly therapy sessions during the course of one
academic year. The client presented his problem as depression, and his
behavior manifested the truth of that self-diagnosis. The sessions generally took the form of discussions about various aspects of the young
man's world: parents, girlfriends, past experiences, and the demands
of graduate school. The client's I-boundary limited the kinds of interactions available in therapy. Classic experimentation was not acceptable. However, the therapist sensed that some significant changes were

taking place in the client. Some behavioral changes were obvious—better grooming, less anxious body movement, better eye contact, for example. Following the summer hiatus from therapy, there was an opportunity to ask the young man for feedback. He said that during the entire 9 months of therapy he had been told, although not directly, that he could trust himself in the choices he made in his interactions with his world. He hadn't believed it at first; late in the school year he finally realized that the therapist had been right. Although the therapist had not been aware of transmitting that belief, the implicit message was the strongest, most meaningful one communicated during those many sessions.

THE THERAPIST AS INSTRUMENT

An emerging trend in Gestalt theory is to concentrate attention on the presence of the therapist in dialogue with the client. In recent years, this concern about the dialogic quality of the therapist-client relationship has sparked new appreciations of the instrumental functions of the therapist (Hendlin, 1987).

The Gestalt therapist is an instrument for change, using all of the artistic skill available to combine perceptions, beliefs, and clinical judgments into a meaningful whole. However, a further condition for change is necessary—presence. It is the basic ingredient in the I-Thou relationship, as described by Buber (1958). The I-Thou experience is contrasted with the I-It interactions that keep the world running, manage relationships, and establish facts and information. While I-It interactions are essential for establishing and maintaining many of the basic elements of the therapeutic relationship, true progress can occur only through the I-Thou interactions. In the transformative experiences of I-Thou, the therapist is a powerful instrument for change.

In spontaneous moments of the I-Thou experience, the therapist and the client become unmediated presences *to each other* through an act of faith (Korb, 1988). From the experience of that presence, personal material that is fresh, new, and spontaneous emerges for a client. The client may explore experiences that are unmediated by any conscious processes of cognitive control. For the therapist, images, ideas, or expressions that can be introduced for personal experimentation surface fresh and clear. Zinker (1977) calls this creative process the "expression of the presence of God in my hands, eyes, brain, in all of me" (p.3). In this intimate contact, there is a sense of unblemished connectedness with all elements of the interaction: an out-of-time, here-and-now presentness that is loving and caring, an absence of critical judgment or evaluation, and an immediate emergence of material for therapeutic use. The Gestalt therapist can be the instrument for such transcendent experiencing in a world of mutuality, actualizing the potential for growth and healing that exists when "two individuals, freely responsible allow their inmost selves to meet" (Jacobs, 1978). Self-repair and self-recuperative systems are empowered in the numinous aura that surrounds persons engaged in such meetings (Korb, 1988).

Every client may not need this kind of healing experience. However, many clients seem almost desperate for experiences of being present, of a connectedness that is not dependency. As an I to a Thou interaction is experienced, the body relaxes, breathing deepens, the voice slows and calms, and eye contact is full of meaning. Love is released so that the moments seem other worldly, out of time and space. The state might be called a healthful, healing, and contactful state of confluence in which aliveness and wholeness are manifest with the therapist as the instrument.

THE THERAPIST AS EDUCATOR

As Yapko (1988) has pointed out, "Therapy may be thought of as first the disruption of dysfunctional patterns, at whatever level the clinician and client deem desirable or necessary, and then the subsequent development of different, more functional patterns" (p. 61). When working with clients who are committed to completing the maturational process, the Gestalt therapist sometimes works as an educator as well as therapist. In this context, an educator is distinguished from a teacher. The teacher instructs and imparts information; the educator stimulates, guides, challenges, and serves as a catalyst (Rogers, 1969). Several Gestalt therapists who have written cogently and extensively about aspects of the therapeutic process have mentioned educational procedures and intentions in the learnings of clients. Zinker (1977) says that creative therapy is "a special form of learning." Polster and Polster (1973) start their book with the assumption that "we [therapists] intend to guide people to a recovery of their contact functions." F. Perls (1947) redefines teaching: "To teach is to show a person that something is possible." In maturational work, such teaching and guidance become critical at times.

Many clients do not know the bodily experience that carries with it the "felt meaning" (Gendlin, 1962) of the truth at that moment. The distinctly physical sense of relief comes with closure of gestalten. To recognize when closure has been achieved, clients must learn the physical manifestations that accompany that moment of expression of personal truth in their insights and awareness. These physical manifestations are unique to each individual: Ellen's stomach rumbled; John experienced his voice as coming from just below his navel; George felt a clear hollow passageway extending through his throat to his stomach; Mary's shoulders relaxed. Learning to recognize the statement of personal truth is a necessary key to all of the maturational work. It moves the work forward with confidence, clarity, and affirmation.

The model for learning in Gestalt therapy is learning by discovery (F. Perls, 1947). What is learned that becomes a part of a system for living must be learned experientially through self-involvement. In many sessions, the therapist suggests activities with which the client may experiment. These experiments are typically presented so as to frame the client's experience in some meaningful way. In effect, they are what Mahatma Gandhi (1949) refers to as "experiments with truth," operations upon one's own experience. These are potential truths that have to be tried out by the individual to see if they fit his or her experience. These experiments are most effective when they provide a framework on which the client may hang the material to be learned. An example of such an experiment is the game known as "May I feed you a sentence?" When the therapist suggests a statement for a client's experimentation, the material in such a sentence exceeds the present awareness of the client and provides a structure for bridging the gap between the client's present awareness and what was emerging as new insights. When the therapist shares an image or an observation, the client may use that material as an experiment with truth to test the emerging gestalten.

The therapist must always use appropriate clinical judgment about the client's dependency needs. When the client is still confronting fears related to being alone or fears about being different in some significant way, any suggestion from a therapist might be used to avoid the experience of the impasse. Only when the client is deemed able to make personal choices is it appropriate to suggest experiments with truth. When functioning as an educator in this sense, the therapist often senses the presence of self-support in the client before the client does. The therapist must rely on judgment at this point, knowing that a client has potentially available healthy functioning and self-support, whether the client is aware of it or not.

In addition to learning to trust their experiences, clients must also learn to think discriminatively. Most clients come to therapy with "either-or" ways of thinking about life events or affective experiences. The therapist may need to confront these self-limiting patterns of thought in the client in order to progress to more integrative experiences. In effect, one client, Art, thought, "Either life experiences fit into my categories or I cannot engage in them." Upon entering therapy, Paul thought about his parents, "Either they must love and appreciate me [an impossibility since they were both dead] or I am not lovable to anyone."

A variation on "either-or" thinking is the "if-then" cognitive strategy, which also forecloses on options. "If I can't succeed in law school, there is nothing left for me." "If this relationship doesn't work out, my life is over." Other signals for such limiting cognitive patterns may be heard in the use of nonqualified, overgeneralized expressions: *all, everyone, no one, never,* and *always.*

In the process of maturation, as a client develops new core concepts or beliefs, the therapist often helps the client express rudimentarily present new beliefs. These beliefs are experienced cognitively at first, and later the individual fully experiences their personal reality. For example, toward the close of therapeutic work, Jane reported, "I know that I am a loving person, but when I saw my mother last week I realized—I *knew*—inside myself that it is true, no matter what she said or did. I am still high from that experience." The movement from being able only to declare her belief and being able to experience it organismically meant that she had fully incorporated a new core construct. Jane had never been able to please her mother and had introjected a belief that she was a hateful person. In therapy, she cognitively clarified her new belief in herself as a loving person; however, experiencing herself as a loving person while being with her mother deepened the reality of this new truth.

FUNCTIONS OF THE THERAPIST

The Therapist as Responder

Developing the Therapeutic Relationship. A delicate balance between personal and professional responsibilities in the therapy relationship becomes apparent as the therapist integrates personal needs while also developing genuine concern and caring about the person who is seeking growth. By sharing perceptions, feelings, experiences, methods, knowledge, and strategies as they contribute to the clarification of the client's processes, the therapist's behavior itself serves as a model of openness, awareness, and acceptance. At the same time, the therapist is able to recognize a client's polarities, barriers to awareness, defenses, movements away from growth, etc., and is able to apply Gestalt therapy strategies appropriately.

Here, we need to clarify one often misunderstood aspect of the therapeutic relationship. When we say "apply Gestalt therapy strategies appropriately," do we mean those appropriate for the therapist or for the client? Is the therapist responsible only for self? Doesn't the therapist have responsibility for the person with whom he or she works? These questions of strategies and responsibility go to the heart of the therapeutic relationship. The answers, to some extent, have to be developed by each individual therapist, but some guidelines can be presented.

Maturation involves the ability to generate self-support. A client may come to therapy looking for someone to provide what is not provided from within, but the goal of therapy is to enable the individual to change such dependent, manipulative behavior. The therapist assumes that within each person lies the necessary personal resources for effective and productive living. Certainly, the therapist should not take responsibility for the client's behavior and attitudes, nor for the use the client makes of the session with the therapist. Thus, the therapist functions as a catalyst for change without taking all of the responsibility for change within the client. Since people are in charge of their own lives, the therapist can possibly educate them in their own responsibility, but the therapist cannot grow or mature for them. To change and to grow is the choice of each client.

Therapists cannot "help" the client in the way that most help is offered (Resnick, 1975). If we attempt to advise or instruct, we will only apply our own answers and awareness to another person's life and experience. Although our answers may be accurate, correct, or beneficial in that they come out of true perception of some situation, they remain ultimately, our answers. Each person has to be able to find answers that are personally true, if the necessary transition from environmental support to self-support is to be made. Ultimately, the therapist is only a resource for the client, a person who may be able to help in the client's personal discovery of the way to awareness.

The Gestalt therapist must be aware of any desire to be a helper and under what circumstances this desire to "help" surfaces. Helping as a means of self-aggrandizement, self-justification, or manipulation is usually destructive in therapy. Even when we have good intentions, the kind of help we have to offer may be suspect. When we affirm each person's uniqueness and ability to generate self-support, we have to discard the notion of having answers for others.

Letting others help themselves affirms the essential value in Gestalt therapy—the presence and worth of self-awareness. The therapist who values self-awareness above personal beliefs and values, above cultural and philosophic biases, undertakes the experience of being a therapist with "respect and acceptance" for the client (Krause, 1977). If what the therapist does has as its ultimate therapeutic expression the client's uniquely experienced movement toward authenticity, the therapist will find that the matters of concern for each client will reach resolution.

Effective interaction between therapist and client is based upon mutual trust. The client must trust the therapist as a professional who is genuinely interested in working with the client, and the therapist must trust the client to be able to integrate the significance of the therapy into the client's personal framework.

Attending to the Obvious. A client's body movements frequently emerge as obviously significant patterns. The therapist may observe, for example, that as a client reports personal experience, the client's voice quality changes, seating posture shifts, or other bodily movement occurs, apparently without conscious design. Such differences often indicate changes occurring within the client, more obvious to the therapist than to the person involved. When the client's movements become the focus of discussion, the therapist can point out what behaviors are being observed, or ask the client to become aware of what is happening gesturally.

A therapist seldom errs in focusing on body language. Most people can construct a wall of words, explanations, rationalizations, and justifications around themselves; the language of the body is obvious, clear, and presents concise data for use in therapy. Simkin (1976) calls these symptoms "truth buttons or truth signals" because they communicate a client's real feelings.

What the client is saying organismically in any situation may be different from what the client thinks is being said. The client's self-report may be inaccurate, consciously or unconsciously, and the therapist who is attending to the total communication will hear a message that the client is unaware of sending. Therefore, attention to the obvious messages is a prime tool of the therapist. Even though, at times, what is obvious to the therapist may be inaccurate "fantasy" or emotional reactions emerging from therapist's own confusion about what is occurring, it is better to voice responses than to quell them. Since the therapist is able to share those moments during therapy, it is possible to use personal observations as a means of establishing contact with the client. If the therapist keeps communications open by reporting personal observations and reactions, the client has the opportunity to experiment with the observations conceptually and to determine if they are appropriate or not.

Seeing Patterns in Therapy. Diagnostic evaluation and history taking may be included in recordkeeping, but they are rarely a part of Gestalt therapy. Yet, there are patterns to be used, when appropriate; that is, there are repeated patterns of behaviors or progressions of psychological states that are lived through by many people. Such scripts or patterns, recognized in a therapy situation, may be used in meaningful ways to help the client; for example, it is useful to the therapist to understand that people often behave incongruently in situations where they experience some amount of threat to their status, to their relationships with others, or to their self-image, for these are important structures in their lives and they will attempt to maintain them. Thus, it would be a mistake to assume that inconsistency or incongruence in one's client is a conscious attempt to avoid what is happening. Knowing about patterns of incongruence may enable a therapist to highlight the client's willingness to explore personal experience fully.

Observations of incongruence between the client's self-report and the therapist's observations can be a productive point of entry for therapy. The therapist reports personal observations without labeling the behavior as "avoidance" or "resistance" and without interpreting the significance. Likewise, when the therapist recognizes a possible pattern underlying the information received from the client, it can be accepted and integrated into the therapist's repertoire without interrupting the therapy process. Since all that the therapist can actually integrate is personal experience and perceptions, he or she can neither integrate nor interpret events for anyone else. Whatever personal meaning is discovered in therapy comes out of the client's own awareness. The therapist, however, does aid in the differentiating processes that precede affirmation and integration.

If we refer to Gestalt learning theory, we see that the "aha" experience, the moment of clear understanding, occurs spontaneously. When the structural relationships of a problem are delineated, when the features are obvious in their functioning and as they relate to the environment and to the client, the understanding emerges in a solid, well formed, and sharply focused pattern or gestalt. Likewise, in therapy, clarity and sharpness come to the therapist out of awareness of the client's habitual patterns for blocking growth.

The therapist can suggest means of differentiating the client's feelings, experiences, and perceptions; however, when that has been accomplished, the client does the rest. At the moment of integration, the client experiences a gestalt completion, a total understanding. Experienced therapists report work in which their understanding of a client's experience and the meaning of what was being done was minimal. Yet, by observing the client's obvious behaviors and working only with the sparse information the client has revealed, the therapist facilitates important understandings and discovers that the integrative work of the client has been accomplished.

In using art work as a therapeutic medium, the therapist may have only sparse information and no cognitive understanding of the content being displayed as the client works, yet therapeutic work is being done.

One of the authors reports working with a female client who was very blocked in verbal descriptions of an inner image that she sensed was very important. The client was given crayons and drawing paper on which she made a series of drawings of the inner image as it changed during the course of an intense, nonverbal 15 minutes. The client experienced closure, but chose not to share it verbally, even at that moment. Thus, the therapist had very little information—observation of the drawings and the process of drawing—when the session ended. Many days later, the client reported that she had become aware of the meaning of the drawing she had made.

It is possible, then, for the therapist to proceed through an effective therapeutic encounter and not know details of the client's problem or even know for sure what the problem was. The client may feel closure and not have cognitions related to the therapeutic activity. Such lack of knowledge does not negate the experience, nor does it deny the therapist's value. It reinforces, however, the concept of clients as having the power in themselves to reach understanding without help from someone else. On the other hand, since the therapist is aware of possible patterns, this professional knowledge may suggest avenues that, with skill and knowledge, enable the exploration of dynamics that otherwise are unapproachable by the client. In addition, the therapist's beliefs and presence help create an environment in which therapeutic activity, without the usual processes of cognition, is possible.

Let us now consider the top dog-underdog dynamic discussed earlier; much therapeutic activity involves creative ways to deal with this polarity. The names for the two poles of intrapsychic activity may be idiosyncratic to the client, but the psychological configurations of a person's making demands upon the self and simultaneously sabotaging efforts to meet those demands, fit conceptualizations of intrapsychic conflict as the most powerful conflict a person may experience. If the therapist sees this possible pattern in the client, an exercise that differentiates the two poles and makes their antipathy explicit may be devised. Once the polarities are clearly differentiated, there is the possibility of resolving the internal conflicts between the two and of freeing energy to be invested in the self, the chooser.

The most relevant and useful patterns to explore in therapy are those, such as top dog-underdog, that block the person from growing and that use energies to maintain neurotic structures rather than for behaviors that are authentic, nonmanipulative, and healthy, as defined in Gestalt terms. Understanding the patterns is important; being able to use them in effective therapeutic interventions is even more important. Usually, the more effective uses involve the presentation of observations of presently occurring processes rather than of conclusions about what is or is not happening. Observations may be used to direct the client's awareness toward some undifferentiated behavior. Conclusions are dangerous; the therapist presumes to know more about the client than the client knows. If someone you know, particularly someone you respect and whose opinions are important, tells you that you are avoiding the issue or that your resistance is showing, that person has drawn a conclusion about your behavior and your motives based only on that person's experience and perceptions. In terms of ill health, that person is projecting personal conclusions on your experience. To state the conclusion permits only responses of acquiescence or rebuttal, both of which turn the encounter into a personal conflict. If you acquiesce in the conclusion, you acknowledge the other person's superiority and may try to change your behavior to fit someone else's opinions. If you argue, you will engage in an encounter in which each participant attempts to justify the disputed perceptions. That kind of encounter between client and therapist is almost always counter-therapeutic.

Observations presented as personal experience and for which the therapist takes full responsibility, however, allow the client to see from the therapist's perspective for a moment, to consider whether the observation is applicable or not. Such observations involve the therapist's awareness of unconscious activity that emerges in nonverbal behavior, or of discrepancies between the verbal and nonverbal behaviors of the client. At best, these observations provide an opportunity for awareness. At worst, the client will deviate from the current experiments; at best, awareness of another person's observations will synthesize old, immobilizing patterns into an understanding accompanied by clarity and a sense of direction.

In order to understand how the client is currently functioning, the therapist should keep in mind the steps in the maturational process. The client's presentation of self demonstrates his or her level of engagement in that process. The therapist's interventions are more cogent and, therefore, more effective when maturational patterns are available in the ground of the therapist's experience. Conceiving work with clients in this framework is both provocative and stimulating. The importance of the metamorphosis related to a changed self-concept and the difficulty of effecting that change, gives the therapist patience and a profound respect for every small change that occurs along the way to self-support.

Therapist as Catalyst

In the course of therapy, many times the therapist maintains a relatively noncontrolling stance wherein the client's present awareness is followed more than the therapist's directions. At such times, the therapist functions more as a catalyst for change than as a responder or director. We will look at some of the catalyst aspects of the therapeutic relationship in the following pages, before turning to the more active and directive roles of the therapist. It is essential that the therapist provide a tone of open, honest, respectful, and trusting interaction with a client; however, such an atmosphere is merely the beginning of growth possibilities. Once the background for the Gestalt experience, the "safe emergency," is established, the therapist is ready to move forward with suggestions for experimentation, to clarify the client's needs, wants, and interests to differentiate areas of confusion or emerging polarities; to remove blocks of personal awareness; to express inner experiences fully; and to help the client choose routes toward health. In addition to all of the above, the therapist deliberately frustrates the client by exposing fantasies and beliefs that maintain repetitious, self-defeating behaviors and those that prevent the client from trying new and possibly more satisfying behaviors. Using personal observations and intuition, the therapist assists the client in making honest expressions of present, personal experience, and frustrates the client's use of old and unproductive patterns. In this last respect, any attempts to play the role of a "good client" are frustrated.

Using appropriate means of frustrating the client's usual ways of avoiding growth and change, the therapist often acts as an agent of awareness. That is, the therapist monitors, observes, and points out client responses on levels different from those of the client; for example, by paying attention to body cues, the therapist often becomes aware of ambivalent responses to which the client is not attuned. The therapist may point out that as the client is saying "yes," body cues are saying "no" or, that a particular verbal response seems to be a key to the client's behavior. The significance of that response then may be explored. In short, the position the therapist holds is informed and perceptive; in working with the client, the therapist communicates a valuing of personal awareness. This usually means teaching processes of awareness explicitly (by offering awareness exercises or directed awareness experiments) or implicitly (by being a model of awareness). Educating the client in personal dynamics provides an opportunity for the client to apply what has been learned during therapy to other areas of the client's life.

The client may learn productive ways of interrupting or frustrating unproductive behavioral patterns. As the therapist works with the unproductive behavior of the client who explores them and discovers the power they are allowed to have, the client begins increased, positive self-monitoring. For example, a client of one of the authors worked on his periodic tendency to pull back from people, to withdraw from those with whom he was close. As this tendency was explored, he became aware of his double messages: in certain situations, he would be communicating "I want you and need you," and at the same time "I want to get away from you." This pattern of withdrawing, while signaling the need to be close, produced confusion and tension between him and his girlfriend. A week after one therapy session in which this pattern had been explored, he reported that awareness of his creating tension had been helpful. As he explained it, the next time he started to slip into his old pattern of behavior he was sufficiently aware of how he was withdrawing to deliberately counteract his own behavior pattern, to frustrate this tendency. On that occasion, instead of withdrawing, he offered to give his girlfriend a back rub. By moving toward her and by increasing contact instead of diminishing it, he broke the unproductive behavior pattern and opened the expression of his caring and desire to be close.

In order to place at the client's disposal useful and appropriate means of becoming aware of dynamic processes, the therapist calls upon Gestalt experiments and strategies that can be introduced effectively. With greater experience and confidence, the therapist can design on-the-spot experiments or modify previous ones situationally. For example, one of the authors worked with a young man who was trying to decide which of two possible job offers he should accept. He was confused, for, although he could logically and rationally list the benefits and disadvantages of each job, he still was unclear about which one he preferred. Obviously, trying to figure out the solution on a purely rational basis had been ineffective. The therapist suggested that he stand with his eyes closed and imagine that he stood at a fork in the road from which paths led to each of the two possible jobs. When he had clearly differentiated their respective characteristics, it was suggested that he allow his body, without deliberation, to move down the path it wanted to travel. There was an almost immediate response. He made definite movement toward one of the choices. His body, as a total organism, knew which path was preferable at that time. This experiment was a useful means of bypassing his intellectualizations about the pros and cons of the choices. Offered to him only as an experiment, it stood as an alternative means of reaching awareness of present desires. After that, it was his own decision to follow the experiment and his decision to accept or reject the results he obtained.

Being open to experimenting and suggesting new ways of approaching an individual's problem means that no set rules or strategies by themselves will suffice in therapy, There are rules, of course, and there are strategies that the therapist should have available, but the rules are sometimes better ignored and the strategies more effective when generated or adapted on the spot and not blindly followed. Like the experienced and knowledgable cook who knows the effect of combining ingredients, the experienced and knowledgable therapist is confident in the novel combinations of experiments devised in sessions with clients. As in the above situation, a therapist may go beyond the superficial strategies when discovering that there are underlying patterns about which one can be cognizant.

Clients often have developed complex and rigid systems for maintaining their unhealthy patterns, and they resist change at the same time they ask for it; they are at an impasse. Change involves risk; it may appear to be moving the person into a new, chaotic, and uncontrolled state. It is often quite threatening. The Gestalt therapist uses suggestions for experimentation that respect the client's fear of change, support the client's being and choices, and also frustrate expectations, fantasies, or other maneuvers that may take the client away from the experience of threat or fear. The Gestalt therapist believes in the ability of all persons to generate within themselves support for effective functioning. The therapist also recognizes that the ability may be buried deeply, and that many persons may choose not to work hard enough or long enough to reach self-support. F. Perls summarizes the issue in this now classic statement: "To suffer one's death and to be reborn isn't easy" (1969, epigraph).

Therapist as Director

While it has been pointed out that the therapist functions primarily as a catalyst for personal growth in therapy by pointing out patterns of avoidance and by calling attention to the client's body language, there are several areas in which the therapist takes more active roles in Gestalt therapy. In particular, the therapist takes the most active roles in directed awareness experiments, in finishing unfinished business, and in breaking through the impasse experienced by the client. We will consider each of these functions in the following sections.

Experimenting. Since awareness is considered to be the *summum bonum* of Gestalt therapy, the therapist often is in a position to provide the necessary experiential focus for the client seeking appropriate routes to growth. Such focusing typically entails methods or strategies of exposing dynamics that occur beneath the client's present level of awareness. This experimenting stage of therapy can be very productive, both in the one-to-one and in the group relationship. It is the exciting stage of discovery about what people are aware of, what to do to clarify inner processes, and how to proceed.

The therapist takes the lead in the experimenting stage by setting up directed awareness experiments, verbal exercises, fantasy trips, body awareness exercises, or interpersonal situations. There may be a particular process the therapist wants to open for exploration, or there may be concerns of the client that may be ready to be explored. Particularly in early group sessions, the therapist may chose to generate large group experiences or dyadic experiences.

In one-to-one therapy, an alternative to trying out structured awareness experiments is merely to begin with suggesting that the client report personal experience from moment to moment, no matter how trivial or confused it may seem to be. This simple technique by itself may be sufficient to lead to the heart of the client's problem. The following experience is an illustration in the way in which awareness experiments can generate clarity.

During a training session in which one of the authors was the therapist, a young woman reported that she was trying to decide if she wanted to work on some problems she was experiencing. She had a large range of possible things to work on and was confused. The therapist asked her to relax with her confusion and see what emerged. After a period of quietness, she reported that she wanted to do something but still did not know what she wanted to do. Again, the therapist asked her to remain with the confusion, not making a decision but merely letting something surface in her awareness. In a few moments she was detailing a series of professional and personal conflicts that disturbed her greatly. None of them seemed to be more important than the others, and her descriptions flowed from one to the other freely. She had obviously thought a lot and talked a lot about the specific problems. Rather than select one of them, or ask her to select one, the therapist suggested that she consider her list of problems as a whole. Initially, she was surprised at the suggestion. However, as she began to consider the suggestion, she saw how she was confusing herself by trying to concentrate on a series of complaints or "problems" in rapid succession, rather than concentrating on the larger gestalt. She also clarified some salient and changeable aspects of the specific situations that troubled her. In this case, what was obvious to the therapist—that there was a common theme in her complaints—was not apparent at all to her. The therapist suggested that the client make a statement regarding the obvious similarities found in all of her complaints. When making such a statement in her own words, the client immediately saw what had been obvious to the therapist for some time. By expressing what was obvious, or "figure," the therapist added information to the situation, and, in effect, helped her to reorganize her perceptual field.

The hallmark of effective directed awareness exercises, whether they are invented at the moment or are part of the therapist's existing fund of strategies, is their clarifying and unifying functions. Just as the therapist may recognize a larger pattern in the client's behavior, the awareness exercises also make it possible for the client to attend to the larger patterns. The therapist's expertise is necessary, however, in order to know what kinds of exercises are appropriate to the situation.

Facilitating Gestalt Completion. Many problems a client faces fall in the category of "unfinished business." The most significant and important unfinished situation calls for immediate attention. In therapy, instead of spending much attention and energy in maintaining or futilely trying to complete incomplete situations, the client can be directed toward an awareness of personal responsibility in the blocking of completion of unfinished business. For example, if a client complains of fatigue, chronic restlessness, or a feeling of helplessness without having a specific idea of how these feelings are being produced, the therapist might suggest that the client "stay with" the feelings of fatigue, give it a voice, or give it a physical identity. If the client verbalizes or pictures the experience of fatigue in meaningful ways, closure regarding the internal and external factors that relate to the fatigue can be reached. Often, it is enough to provide momentary clarity for the client to be able to proceed toward resolution; the therapist may not need to intervene directly.

The therapist may also facilitate bringing the client's unconscious, unfinished situations to conscious awareness by using Gestalt exercises as springboards to more concentrated work. For example, a potent group exercise (Enright, 1976), involves simple projection on the part of each member. The therapist may have a box of children's toys and games, which is dumped on the floor in the middle of a group. Each person is instructed to find one piece that looks most interesting or absorbing. After allowing enough time for the selection process, the therapist then suggests that each person report to the group what the experience of being that toy is like. The experience of projecting oneself into an object and detailing experiences from that perspective often brings out feelings associated with unfinished episodes.

Body language, the physical cues perceived by the therapist, may indicate movement toward completing situations. Even when the person maintains control over thinking and does not allow, into consciousness, the need to reach closure, the body will still be seeking that resolution. On several occasions, we have witnessed a client begin a session with merely a physical experiential description of bodily sensations, then gradually move toward discovering personal responsibility for a headache, a backache, or an upset stomach. The physical symptom may be a real, continuing, coping response the client is un-

willing to surrender, because it has served so well. There are also occasions when the situation that prompted the response has, in fact,
ended, but the mechanism persists almost automatically. This persis-
tent behavior then becomes the target, and the therapist directs the
client to become aware of what is being done physiologically. The residual coping mechanism needs to be brought to awareness so the client
can then choose whether or not to discontinue it.

Many people, for example, have learned to retroflect, restraining their
words by clenching their jaws; even in situations where they no longer
need to be censoring their responses, the clenched jaw remains. Some
people exhibit this symptom so strongly they hardly open their mouths
when they speak. Tightened jaws may be inappropriate in present
therapeutic situations, but they either indicate that there is much that
still needs to be expressed or that this mode of physical response has
become habitual. Awareness of the "symptom" of tight jaws can lead
to whichever closure is appropriate for the client.

Although learning to control a "symptom" cannot replace actually
dealing with the underlying process and completing the targeted incomplete gestalt, an understanding of the dividing line between dealing with symptoms that persist beyond old situations and symptoms
arising from current experiences makes it possible for the therapist to
attend appropriately to the client's experiences.

With the completion of even a small piece of unfinished business,
the individual experiences a sense of fulfillment. Present experience is
heightened whenever one is able to complete a past experience, for the
energy tied up in the past then becomes freed and available for the
present and the future. Although one may have many important unfinished situations and work on only one of them, the experience of completing gives the client a sense of competence and the ability to complete other situations. As one unfinished situation is resolved, increasing
energy is released for dealing with other situations.

Working Through an Impasse. A client who comes into therapy is at an
impasse. That is, as F. Perls (1969) defines it, the client is at the point
where environmental support is no longer available, and authentic self-
support has not yet been achieved. It is likely that there are catastrophic expectations about what is beyond that point, or there is such
a complicated system of avoidance, the client actually cannot know what
is expected and may be disoriented, confused, hesitant, and ambivalent. This kind of experience may also occur many times in the course
of therapy as a client reaches the end of what is known and safe, regardless of the emotional content, while further exploration is seen as
hazardous. A client may consciously draw the line beyond which the

therapeutic encounter may not go, and the therapist may elect to respect that line and wait for future developments.

F. Perls (1969) notes that the impasse is "the crucial point in therapy, the crucial point in growth." Ruth Cohen (1970) states that con-
ceptualization of the impasse is F. Perls' unique and most important
contribution to psychotherapy. The therapist, having worked with the
client toward recognition and removal of prior environmental manipulations for support, can help the client discover a route through the
point of the impasse by aiding in the generation of organismic support.
In general, the therapeutic technique is to concentrate on the impasse
itself. With active resistance, the therapist asks the client to experience
the impasse in terms as complete as possible. Procedures that keep the
client in the present and make it clear that the therapist is sensitive to
everything going on may minimize the fear of change. The therapist
needs to maintain two levels of awareness: awareness of the totality of
what is occurring moment to moment, and a specific awareness of the
details and patterns of the client's responses. Movement through the
impasse may be difficult for the therapist, if he or she is solely aware
of the client's perceptions at that point. That is, if the therapist becomes confused or sees only the verbal, logical, or abstracted conflicts
the client sees, the therapist and client may become locked in a strug-
gle for control, which will certainly become counter-productive.

At the impasse, the most obvious, and often the simplest configuration or movement is most serious and important; it is the key to
movement through the impasse. When the therapist is aware of confusion it becomes the obvious configuration to be dealt with and will
lead to the next awareness and the next. When the therapist is able to
direct the client to the impasse itself and to how the client blocks progress, the therapist opens the way for movement out of the situation
and into the world of experience beyond the impasse.

A dramatic example occurred as one of the authors was working
with a young woman who, being at a major decision-making point in
her life, needed to create distance between herself and certain people
she perceived as making demands on her. She experimented with ways
of telling them that she needed some space, yet she was not straightforward verbally and she felt unsuccessful and dissatisfied. After experimenting with several approaches to making clear her underlying
demands, the therapist became aware that it was the verbalization itself that held her back from dealing with these people. Her thinking
and her words undercut the force and power of her feelings, and she
would alter her demands to fit her thinking. At that point, the therapist suggested that she act out her feelings, doing to his outstretched
arms what she wanted to do to the people in her life. She proceeded

to wrestle furiously with the therapist, transferring her blocked words into actions and releasing the pent-up energy she had in the situation. The impasse was broken through at that moment.

Another way of dealing with an impasse is illustrated in the first transcribed therapy session (Appendix A). Rather than stay with the client's moment-by-moment awareness, the therapist, in this situation, chooses to suggest that the client shift attention to a more objective perspective in order to become aware of the internal, conflicting forces that are impacted. A breakthrough is facilitated in this way. These two different processes, both effective in dealing with impasses, again indicate that there is no "right" way to interact therapeutically with a client.

Some people come to therapy not to change but to justify their present behaviors or to show their power by frustrating others. When a therapist believes that the client is being manipulative, when there is the feeling of frustration or anger, the therapist can give feedback regarding these feelings without placing the responsibility on the client. Similarly, when the therapist is confused, it is best to admit it. The client may have unconsciously engineered the confusion as an avoidance technique. Clear, honest, and straightforward therapist behavior is essential; the basic truth that evolves in the client-therapist relationship demands that the client see the therapist as a real and authentic person. The therapist's feedback restructures the situation constructively, being expressed descriptively and with responsibility for one's own behavior, instead of making another responsible for it.

SUMMARY

As the Gestalt therapist develops in therapeutic work, the awareness that idiosyncratic experiences of clients do not always "go by the book" becomes internalized. Many cases do not fit a stated methodological perspective. If the therapist tries to concentrate only on dynamics that fit stated patterns, he or she may sacrifice the client's best interests. Therefore, methods alone are not enough; they are modified and mediated by thorough training and extensive day-to-day experiences in therapeutic encounters. Experience brings a validation of sidetracks, detours, or changes in the context, and it ultimately contributes an ease and sensitivity to the subtleties, as well as to the special, momentary whole of any situation. Ease, sensitivity, and creative instincts develop in beginning therapists as they find ways of handling Gestalt therapy that best fit their own personalities and styles, always keeping in mind the phenomenological perspective and radical respect for all aspects of every client.

The possibility for deep and powerful therapeutic work inherent in the Gestalt therapy system, as illustrated in the transcripts in the appendices, demands that therapists be well trained, whether certificated or not; be very clear about themselves, their perceptions, values, their ethical stance, and therapeutic tools; be knowledgable about gestalt theory and technique; and be able to creatively apply any learnings and spontaneous designs for experimentation appropriately. The system also demands that clients choose therapists with great care.

Responding to the present, its wholeness as well as its constantly emerging figures, is an invaluable ability in any therapist, and even more necessary in Gestalt therapy; awareness of the present is one of the basic processes that both the therapist and the client need for intense, powerful, and healing therapy to take place. With the development of present-centered awareness, the capacity for an I-Thou experience, a good theoretical roadmap, and therapeutic tools, the therapist and client move on their separate journeys toward personal growth and fulfillment.

Afterword

In the 1980 edition of this book, we stated that we had "stopped the time, made a crosscut through our experiences, and share with you what we know, believe, perceive, and imagine at this time . . . October 1979." In 1988, we followed a similar process, including comments on the impact of the experiences in the intervening years. However, Gestalt therapy is not, and has never been, static. Thus, in 1988, an afterword is necessary. There are some general trends of great importance as well as of on-going practical and theoretical interest to the Gestalt community.

EXTENSION OF GESTALT
THERAPY INTO NEW DOMAINS

In some ways the current conceptualizations of the therapeutic enterprise have caught up with Gestalt therapy. From the beginning, we have seen humans as whole organisms containing parts that interact in dynamic ways, rather than as a sum of parts that function together in a more mechanistic fashion. In 1988, the holistic point of view is being increasingly accepted as integral to body/mind theory and research. Healing is seen as one of the processes of a whole and dynamic individual. The conception of the individual as always being in a process of interacting with the environment has been incorporated into new approaches to therapy and in revisions of long-standing approaches. Gestalt therapists, themselves, are in process of elucidating, more cogently than in the past, the significance of dynamics and processes in terms of on-going therapy.

Reports of the practice of Gestalt therapy are increasing. Attention is being paid to Gestalt therapists who treat populations other than "normal neurotic" adults. Descriptions of Gestalt therapy with couples, families, sex offenders, and batterers are emerging. Oaklander

(1978), for example, has described a Gestalt therapy approach to children and adolescents. Additionally, Gestalt therapy has been described as being found effective with such populations as profoundly disturbed persons (Stratford and Brallier, 1979), schizophrenic patients (Gagnon, 1981), and sexually impotent males (Harman, 1979). Transcripts of actual therapy sessions, such as a recent transcript by Aylward (1988), are also being presented for review and reaction in *The Gestalt Journal*, reflecting an increased desire on the part of the Gestalt community to look closely at the unique contributions Gestalt therapy makes to ongoing therapy.

Gestalt therapy is based on a set of principles of personal functioning, as well as principles of interactional behavior. The principles are translatable into settings other than outpatient or group psychotherapy. One example of such a translation into psychotherapy in the classroom (Shub, 1981) has added to the understanding of the range of settings to which Gestalt therapy processes may be applied. Also, organizational behavior has been explored from a Gestalt perspective (Brown, 1986).

Theoretical issues have been figural throughout the decades of Gestalt therapy practice. As therapists practice with differing populations and as new foci emerge in the therapy community as a whole, a healthy need for theoretical integration has resulted in encounters among theoreticians. For example, the entire Fall 1988 issue of *The Gestalt Journal* is devoted to theoretical issues of import to many practicing Gestalt therapists. Current emphasis among certain Gestalt therapists on healing processes and on spirituality in psychotherapy have stirred the Gestalt community and will assuredly continue to excite debate and promote serious reflection among practitioners and theorists alike.

As theoretical issues are brought to the forefront of Gestalt practice, certain perceived deficiencies in Gestalt theory become even more important. There is, for example, the tendency for others to see Gestalt therapy as a limited set of techniques for increasing awareness of the client. The richness and versatility of Gestalt therapy has been overlooked because of oversimplified accounts of the theory and because of a tendency to categorize Gestalt therapy processes into a list of interventions to be applied without reference to the context in which they have been successful.

It has been noted on many occasions that a weakness of Gestalt therapy is that there is no fully developed, well-articulated developmental theory to accompany the therapy processes themselves. Major therapies generally contain explanations of the development of the individual and the forces that exert positive and negative influences on the growth of healthy and unhealthy functioning. Although many therapists and theorists would agree that there is an implicit developmental theory in the early writings of Gestalt therapy (Brown et al., 1988), such as described by F. Perls et al. (1951), a more accessible and more contemporaneous exigesis of developmental principles is needed in the Gestalt literature.

Along with a concern for completing the unfinished theoretical work, there appears to be a surge of interest among some elements of the Gestalt therapy community to mainstream Gestalt therapy (Brown et al., 1988). A movement toward greater exposure of the therapy would enable therapists within and without the Gestalt community to share their understandings of the therapeutic processes and the basis for their success. While Gestalt therapy does share several important assumptions and understandings with other therapies (see chapter 4), the unique, practical and theoretical contributions of Gestalt therapy have not been realized outside the Gestalt community as completely as they should.

Growth of dynamic and holistic understandings from therapy orientations other than Gestalt therapy are now being documented in the current literature. This growth of theory sometimes leads to the presentation of ideas that are also buried among the early Gestalt therapy theoretical writings, or that are implicit in its practice. Gestalt therapy runs the risk of being forgotten among this therapy growth simply because it has not documented dynamics and processes as fully as have proponents of other therapy approaches. The need for members of the Gestalt community to write for publications other than *The Gestalt Journal*, and, in so doing, to extend the theoretical boundaries of Gestalt therapy is evident (Miller, 1988).

A further, especially exciting trend concerns the international flavor of the community of Gestalt therapists. Gestalt therapy is being practiced in more and more countries, leading eventually to significant changes in practice and theory. The 1988 Annual Conference, held in Montreal, provided simultaneous translations of presentations from English to French and from French to English. In 1989, *The Gestalt Journal* will include for the first time papers from other than writers in English. These articles will be translated into English, as well as presented in the native language of the writers. The international nature of scholarly exchange related to Gestalt therapy will surely open greater vistas for therapists and theorists alike, allowing for the inclusion of voices from outside the English-speaking world and for dialogue related to therapy issues that transcend national boundaries.

ISSUES REGARDING TRAINING

The term *Gestalt therapist* used in this book is a generic term that indicates an expert in the philosophy, the theory, and the practice of Gestalt therapy. An expert is one who is well grounded, well trained and has had enough experience to have become a creative artist in therapy. Obviously, this description does not fit all therapists who call themselves Gestalt oriented. Beginning therapists may have been attracted to this orientation for a number of reasons. Erving and Miriam Polster (Hycner, 1987) have noted that the "armamentarium" of Gestalt therapy is beguiling, the strategies and the sense of presence are attractive, and the temptation to follow technical formulations slavishly can be nearly irresistible. However, it must be clear at this point that to handle such methods and such power effectively demands an extended period of training, continuous personal work with an expert therapist, and extensive practice under the supervision of an expert.

Issues regarding the training of therapists have been important to the Gestalt community because of a concern that those who profess to be Gestalt therapists should be well-grounded in its theory and practice. Concerns about Gestalt training methods, models, and personnel have been voiced regularly at conferences and within *The Gestalt Journal* (Brown et al., 1987). At the 1988 Annual Conference on the Theory and Practice of Gestalt Therapy, a panel composed of all editors of *The Gestalt Journal* indicated their concerns as they addressed the "novices" in the audience. Since there is no set of guidelines for training and there appears to be no movement to formulate and adopt such guidelines, concern over the adequacy of training procedures will continue.

At the present time, several institutions offer Gestalt therapy training, not only in the United States but in many countries around the world—Brazil, Canada, England, France, Germany, and Japan, for example. Such institutions are listed in the annual *Gestalt Directory*, published by The Center for Gestalt Development, Highland, New York, which also lists individual therapists who have chosen to be listed therein. No set of guidelines has been adopted universally. However, trainers are aware of their responsibility for the three aspects of training just noted: strong theoretical grounding, intense personal Gestalt work, and extended supervised practice.

Beginning therapists need strong role models and intensive training followed by supervised opportunity to move away from the model in order to discover a personal style and set of personal methods. F. Perls states that there are rules that must be learned, and then may be broken. Breaking the rules may be done with sufficient experience and with the clear personal channels founded on self-differentiation and unrelenting respect for the selfhood of both client and therapist.

There appears to be a consensus within the Gestalt community that prospective therapists be trained to high levels of professional and personal functioning. Further issues regarding the training of Gestalt therapists will undoubtedly receive increasing attention as Gestalt therapy continues to grow and to demonstrate its effectiveness with a wide range of clients and in a wide variety of settings.

Appendices

Transcripts of
Two Therapy Sessions

In these appendices we present transcripts of two actual therapy sessions with comments (in italics) concerning the stages in the therapeutic process, the therapists's interventions, and the clients's experiences, as indicated by his verbal and nonverbal responses. The sessions are presented as they actually happened, with only minor editing to enhance readability. Each represents a different kind of Gestalt therapy interaction. In the first session, the names of the client, his daughter, and places mentioned remain intact; this is in accord with the client's wish to help others understand his experience in the loss of his daughter and in the therapeutic interaction that brought him relief. In the second session, the client's name has been changed; he is a young professional counselor. The first session (Appendix A) illustrates the classic Gestalt process of gestalt completion; the second session (Appendix B) illustrates the dialogic Gestalt process of exploration.

APPENDIX A:
GESTALT COMPLETION

Step One: Expression

(Therapist takes charge, suggests that client take time to experience rather than report at the overt verbal level.)

(Note: "C" is client; "T" is therapist.)
C: What I want to do is set up the situation.
T: (Interrupting) I'd like you to first stop and let yourself settle—take a minute and whenever you feel ready, begin.
C: (Pause of a couple of minutes—deep sigh) About 2 months ago my daughter died, and she's been dying for 4 or 5 years, and I've not been able to get the feelings going and . . . and know that there is some

137

guilt and some anger, but I couldn't handle her telling me that she didn't want to live (begins to cry).

(Therapist supports and encourages expression of feelings.)

T: Yes, just allow your feelings to come . . . .
C: I have a real philosophy that says whatever happens to me I caused and I am . . . deeply believing in spiritual/mind healing. And I wanted to work with her but she didn't believe this, so I knew for me it was impossible to go to her until she called (holding back tears).

(Therapist again suggests that feelings are okay. It seems that blocked feelings may be the target for the session.)

T: Allow those feelings to come.
C: (Crying) She never called . . . I get so goddamn mad . . .

(Therapist believes that the scene is set, that the client is experiencing rather than reporting. The client is now ready to experiment. The therapist makes it clear that the client is in charge and has choices about how to proceed.)

T: I'd like to check with you about how you'd like to deal with this.
C: Oh, I haven't the slightest idea, but I do know that there was a lot of ego connected with the fact that she was number one daughter and was a very attractive thing and just wonderful. To have her check out . . . and, of course, the last memories I had of her were so awful, so absolutely terrible.

Step Two: Differentiation

(Therapist suggests an experimental dialogue.)

T: Do you feel ready to talk to her now, to bring her here in your fantasy?
C: I suppose . . . I, I . . . .

(Therapist keeps client in touch with present experience, encouraging the expression of awarenesses.)

T: Where are you right now?
C: Well, I'm both ways. I'm, I know that I didn't say good-bye to her. I'm really not aware that she's gone, that she's dead. I don't believe that I've accepted that at all. I imagine . . . I expect that I'll go to Santa Barbara and she'll be there.

(Therapist attempts to focus the dialogue, keeping the client in charge.)

T: Would you be willing to tell her this? Does that feel right to you?
C: Ah . . . I suppose . . . yes.

(Therapist continues to check client's willingness to proceed and suggests that the client take a major part in structuring the dialogue.)

T: However it is more comfortable, with your eyes open or your eyes closed. Take a minute to see her, visualize her . . . when you're ready, begin with whatever you have to communicate to her.

C: (pause) Kathy . . . (T: Yeah) (C begins to cry)

C: I can't believe that you're not here. I'm really sorry that I didn't say good-bye to you—that it didn't seem to be the right time; and when I saw you last you were so . . . so drugged . . . so different . . . so terrible . . . goddamn it, why didn't you . . . (breaks into sobs).

T: Yeah . . . .

C: Why didn't you say something? Why didn't you try to fight it?

(Therapist intensifies the experience.)

T: (repeating client's words) Why didn't you say something? Why didn't you try to fight it?

C: You kept going from remedy to remedy—this was going to do it and that was going to do it, and I got so angry with you. I can't help it. I should have been able to accept you as you were. It's so difficult . . . (sobs)

T: Yeah.

C: Oh, God, it's difficult (sobbing) . . . it hurts so . . . God almighty!

(Therapist suggests differentiating the feelings and focusing them outward toward the daughter.)

T: Check with yourself and see if you are willing to share some of that hurt, anger, and resentment with her.

C: Yeah . . . you just checked out and left the rest of us here, goddamn it. (sobbing) Life was so good for you. Of course, how would I know for you, but gee, wow, you never had anything tough happen in your life. Life was served up to you on a silver platter with gold around the edges. I resented the fact that you were so damned dependent; you knew that your mother would pay your bills, do anything you wanted, jump through a hoop for you. And all the time she was killing you . . . and that got me angry. If you would have had to face your situation with your income, you'd either have to shit or get off the pot . . . and you refused to see that all of this dependency was bringing the family around that last scene. I was so angry—here you were on the bed, your brother was trying to placate you, the nurse was there offering you melon balls you wanted or some other things that had to be brought from Hong Kong or around the world—your mother was there—and you were continually wanting more—wanting more—everybody was around. Why, Louis XIV didn't have such an attentive court as you had there—and it got me so fucking angry to see that and to see her.

(Therapist keeps the expression focused and suggests some exaggeration.)

T: Tell her that.

C: Goddamn it, how could you do that? How could you manipulate the whole fucking family? Your brothers were there, not knowing what they were looking at, not realizing they were looking at slow suicide, and you were asking for it, you were asking for every goddamn bit of it!

(Therapist suggests more clarity about the underlying process to encourage overt expression of any remaining feelings.)

T: Check out about her manipulation of you and see if that fits. How is she manipulating you in all of this?
C: Yeah . . . you did it. I made a trip all the way down to Tijuana and you hardly even said "boo" to me. And I just was so hurt inside, and you were the Queen Bee and nobody else was having any problem, like I wasn't having to move to a new city and a new house. You didn't give a shit about anybody else. It was me . . . me . . . me . . . poor me. You had a goddamn terminal case of poor little me. That really pissed me off . . . a lousy, lousy attitude, Kathy . . . (pause)

(Therapist checks to see if any feelings need to be expressed.)

T: See if there is anything else you want to say to her right now about this—about your anger, feeling manipulated.

(Client begins to discriminate among the feelings.)

C: . . . Well, of course, I did see the other side of it. I could see that your brothers were at least getting in touch with their emotions and . . . but . . . they didn't know what they were seeing, they were supposedly seeing a woman with great courage . . . and you, John, you were in charge of the morphine and codeine and opium and all the rest of the stuff . . . the pills and the injections and the tablets and the whole bunch of stuff . . . (pause)

(Therapist suggests experiment to clarify the polarization of the feelings as the client has experienced them.)

T: Okay. What I'd like you to do if you are willing, is to—now—just allow yourself to let go of these feelings, and I'd like you to shift and become Kathy and let her respond to you.
C: Oh, God . . . Oh, God. . . .
T: Are you willing to do that?
C: I'll try it . . . sheewww. . . .

(Therapist suggests bodily change to help clarify the polarized feelings.)

T: And, if you can, I think it would be really helpful if you shifted positions. Move over there. (Ken changes positions . . . pause) Take a little time to feel what it feels like to be Kathy.
C: . . . (begins to sob deeply)

(Therapist lends physical support in the critical point in the experiment.)

T: Yeah . . . (moves physically closer to Ken)
C: It feels like shit . . . Oh God . . . how much hurt.
T: See if you can be there and experience that . . . What did you call Ken? Dad, or . . . ?
C: Oh, Dad . . . Oh Dad . . . I know you're not interested in the way I feel. I know you're condemning me. I know you didn't believe in my route—I feel as if I'm alone. I like the Mexicans down in Tijuana and I have fun down there. Dr. Carerra is my friend and the other doctors and nurses. I love to talk with them; they are good people. They want to help me. But you . . . sure you came down, and I'm sorry that I wasn't—it was one of my low days and I didn't talk to you—and you were talking a mile a minute to Mary, and you two were having so much fun . . .

(Therapist slows the work down so that the daughter's statements may be experienced clearly.)

T: Would you tell Dad that again?
C: I'm sorry that I couldn't go your route, Dad. I was on a different route. I was on a different route. (chokes on the words)
T: . . . Tell him more about that.
C: I didn't know why I had this feeling of hopelessness. My relationship with Bob hadn't worked out very well. It didn't seem to have any direction; I didn't seem to know what I wanted to do, where I wanted to go, what I wanted to accomplish. And it seemed to me so much more safe to just stay in the nest and let mother pay my bills and be incorporated in her sphere. I did enjoy sort of organizing the International Association of Cancer Victims and Friends, planning their affairs and writing their circulars, but basically I guess I just didn't feel . . . I just felt like I was in a dead end, that there was no real direction, no real reason for me to be . . . And I guess that was hard for you to understand. . . . (breathes heavily)

Step Three: Affirmation

(Therapist tries to clarify the verbal statement and elicit the feelings associated with the heavy breathing.)

T: What's that?
C: Hard to understand (cries). . . . God almighty, it was hard to understand.

(Therapist senses that the client has moved away from the role of daughter. He follows the client's process and suggests a role shift.)

T: All right, shift position. Come back and be Ken. I think you have shifted roles.
C: Yeah. . . .

(Therapist slows the work so that the client may experience deeply.)

T: I'd like you just to be still a minute. Close your eyes and just review
     what she has told you, what she has said . . . and receive that . . .
C: (begins to cry)

(Therapist suggests the affirmation of the deep feelings.)

T: Just allow that to happen.
C: (Crying) I didn't understand! I didn't understand it! It doesn't make
     any sense at all—no goddamn sense. . . .
T: Yeah, no sense at all. . . .
C: There isn't any sense to that . . . (cries) . . . no sense to that . . .
     it doesn't make any sense! (blows nose)

(Therapist encourages the client's congruent statement, the central experience.)

T: Can you share that with her?
C: (more composed) I didn't understand that, Kathy.
T: Yeah. . . .
C: I just didn't understand that . . . I'm sorry it just doesn't make any
     sense.

*(Therapist suggests verbal clarification of what the client has said, the completion
of the verbal statements.)*

T: Can you be more specific with her about . . . how it doesn't make
     any sense. . . .

(Client begins to clarify both poles of the father-daughter interaction.)

C: Well, yes. You're a beautiful girl with tremendous potential . . . just
     the way you related to those Mexicans made me so pleased, and you
     were so pleased to be able to speak to them in their own idiom. So
     much conversation—I remember how you told me that you went to a
     dance with your current boyfriend who was a Mexican, and you sud-
     denly realized and he suddenly realized that you were the only gringo
     in the outfit, the only Anglo in the whole room and nobody realized
     it. And I was so pleased, it seemed like you could make something out
     of that. And then I remember, too, a clinic in Santa Barbara that was
     treating the migrant workers, and you had so much fun there 'cause
     you were able to talk to them and you were able to translate, able to
     help them. And you didn't denigrate them, you didn't judge them,
     you didn't treat them as inferiors. You just had some really great things
     going. I was excited for you and . . . I don't know. . . I just don't
     know.

(Therapist asks the client to complete the thought.)

T: What is it that you don't know?
C: I didn't know that that wasn't a calling, a direction . . . why couldn't

you make something out of that? Why wasn't that fun? Why wasn't that a reason for living, a reason for moving? A reason—you know damn well that anything that you'd wanted, anything you'd wanted in a way of education or travel or anything—your mother would have given you just like that. (snaps fingers) So it wasn't that you were in some sort of poverty box. You just had no goddamned excuse at all for copping out. What you did, you copped out on us and that's a shitty thing to do. You just gave up, rolled over. That doesn't feel good to me at all.

(Therapist structures the dialogue.)

T: Okay, if it feels right I would like you to shift and be Kathy again and respond to Dad.

C: (sighs and shifts position)

(Therapist takes care that the client experience as deeply as possible so there will be a minimum of unfinished business.)

T: And, again, take just a minute to listen to what Dad has said, how he doesn't understand.

C: (pause) Well, Dad, I did have fun. I did have fun at the intensive language school. And I did have fun relating to . . . Oh, well, you remember when I was working in the kitchen in a Mexican restaurant in Santa Barbara and the Mexicans there were my friends. I did have fun there. And I was able to understand their jokes, and their life, and their feelings. And I didn't know why it wasn't enough. I don't know why my affection for the Tijuana group wasn't enough. You remember when I served down there as a medical assistant without pay and was able to again be a helper in the clinic. I remember how proud I was when I told you that all the clinic felt that I was their baby. You remember when you came down there to surprise me and you asked for me in Spanish, and they didn't know who you wanted, but as soon as you said my name everybody said, oh yes! We know where she is, and that was so pleasing to me. In the middle of that anthill they knew where I was and they knew all about me. All the nurses, all the doctors, I was their baby. And then I got pregnant and then the problem was, would it be possible to have the baby . . . and cancer . . . and everybody down in Tijuana was pulling for me. They really wanted me to have that baby. And I aborted it somehow . . . and I was sad . . . but I guess I just didn't get it together.

(Therapist tries for closure on this part of the interaction.)

T: Is there something more you can tell your Dad to help him understand?

C: (pause) Just . . . I don't know, Dad . . . I guess I just felt that several of these past years I was marking time, trying to get direction, and somehow it just didn't ever come. And it was so easy to just relax and sleep late in the morning and not have any plan or direction . . . anybody expecting anything from me. I guess I just wanted the easy route.

I don't have any explanation. . . . I don't know. My boyfriends were very solicitous. My ex-husband, even a boyfriend of years gone by visited me. And I was pleased to have that concern. Just got that hopeless feeling . . . I know that you sent me a letter telling me that, whereas you accepted my position, that you wanted me to know what your position was without any condemnations, and I guess I was glad to hear that . . . (pause)

(Therapist senses that the dialogue has reached an impasse and suggests a different experiment to facilitate focus and to move the client through.)

T: Okay, Ken, if you're willing I would like to shift a little bit and try something, a different stance. What I would like you to do is to become Ken's objective self—the objective, compassionate, loving observer part of you—and look at Dad and Kathy there and see what you see. Look at what has happened from that perspective. Does that seem right?
C: Yeah, yeah. . . .

(Therapist structures the new material so that the client may be as clear as possible, so that the client may affirm his experience.)

T: You might want to take a different place or stand or whatever feels right to you. (Ken moves to a different place where he can see the two places he had sat in earlier.) Take some time to get yourself into that loving, objective place.

(Client begins to affirm the truth of the two positions in a dialogue.)

C: (pause . . . deep breaths . . .) Well, I see Kathy and I know that she did the best that she could do with what she understood.
T: Um . . . hmmm.
C: She did the best she could. That's hard to say . . . Oh, that's hard to say (crying) . . . Oh . . . she did the best she could. And I guess Ken did the best he could.

(Therapist anchors the experience in the present so the client may experience congruence.)

T: Imagine yourself looking at Ken, and say that to him.
C: (pause) Yeah, I really think I can say, Ken, that you did what you could. It wasn't very much . . . it wasn't very much. (cries)

(Therapist keeps the role clear.)

T: Does that feel objective? I'm just checking.
C: Yes, sure it does. (crying) It wasn't very much.
T: I am concerned that you are doing some judging, and I want to make sure that you stay objective.
C: Yeah, it's tough . . . (in a deeper voice) . . . and I guess Kathy didn't really feel that you could do anything for her healthwise. (Client

begins to see clear differentiation between father and daughter positions.) I know, Ken, you feel that you could have opened up the healing power within her . . . had she wanted it . . . and I can see Kathy,
who felt that cobalt was a route, chemotherapy again was a possible
route but it was too terrible for her physically and that she felt that her
. . . she actually felt that her vegetarian diet would cure her. And
every couple of weeks she had a new diet. And I guess you couldn't
quite understand that, Ken. You wouldn't get that so it was tough for
both of you to relate in the later stages . . . there wasn't too much to
talk about. You really weren't tuned in on the same wavelength. (Client
sees clear differentiation.) I guess I can see that now—on different
wavelengths—and all you could do that last day for that 2 hours that
you were with her was to sit there and be absolutely amazed . . . and
frustrated . . . and sad . . . all at the same time . . . (Client affirms
personal experience objectively.) So I guess you, too, did what you
could, Ken, with what you knew.
T: Uh-huh.
C: And I guess you were smart not to press yourself or your ideas on
her but just to agree that you could to accept her and let her go. But
. . . but . . .

(Therapist keeps the differentiation clear, and begins to check for closure.)

T: Just check again and be sure that you are centered and objective, and
see if there is anything more you want to communicate to either one
of them.
C: . . . Well, I know, Ken that you were . . . after being with her that
last time, you were glad that she went quickly. She was in terrible,
terrible pain. And that's why I guess you weren't able to get in touch
with a lot of sadness at the funeral. I know that the funeral was a very
exciting time for you . . . probably one of the biggest days in your
whole life. (Client continues to affirm personal experience objectively)
but I can see why you weren't able to get in touch with all the sadness
and all the frustration at the time. And maybe we are not really able
to cope with your not ever seeing her again . . . (sighs)

(Therapist suggests process for completion of the differentiation process.)

T: Whenever you feel ready, I'd like you to shift back to being Ken,
Dad, in your original place. And again take some time to receive.
C: (Pause) Yeah, it was hard to—it is hard, in the present, to believe I
won't see her again. (pause)

(Therapist checks into immediate experience.)

T: What is going on inside of you right now?
C: Oh, I'm just thinking about that . . . it's (crying softly) . . . it doesn't
seem possible. It still doesn't make any sense (sobbing). (Client makes
clear congruent statement.) It still doesn't make any sense.
T: Yeah.
C: I don't know if it ever will. . . .

Step Four: Closure

(Therapist suggests an experiment to discover unfinished business in the dialogue.)

T: Just an idea. I wonder if you would go back to Kathy and say something like, "Kathy, I still haven't accepted that you're dead," or whatever seems right to you.

(Client is resistant to the suggestion)

C: You mean to be her?
T: No, to talk to her and tell her that you haven't accepted that she's gone.
C: (sigh) (pause . . . crying) Kathy, honey, you just can't believe how tough it is to believe that you're not coming back. Oh, (sobs) that's impossible.

(Therapist suggests statement that may fit.)

T: Yeah, and try out, "and that's what is so hard for me to understand."
C: Yeah, that makes it really tough—really, really tough . . . it is really tough for me to admit that you aren't coming back. That has been a real hard place.
T: Uh-huh.
C: A real hard place. And maybe you can understand that.

(Client brings out unfinished business from the past that contaminates the present experience.)

C: And, I guess too, Kathy, that you've got to remember that . . . that I think that I have some guilt that when your mother died and I divorced, that I wasn't able to do for you. Especially when you moved out of town, you moved to Santa Barbara, and oh, I just felt terribly isolated and rejected by the whole group, and it wasn't your fault, and I guess it wasn't anybody's fault, but . . . so I guess I felt, I felt guilty that there were some things that might have been done that I didn't do. (Client affirms what seems true.) That probably is an added difficulty here in this situation.

(Therapist suggests a process for closure.)

T: Okay, Ken, time is getting close to the end. What I would like you to do is stay in contact with Kathy right now. And I'd like you to say goodbye to her in some way, realizing that you can come back to her in fantasy again, or tell her that you will come back—whatever feels right. Say goodbye to her for now, and maybe tell her something of what you still have to deal with in relation to her and what you have done in this session.

C: (pause) Well, Kathy, I do want to . . . whew . . . I do want to say goodbye to you and I want you to know that it's . . . it's been very difficult for me to do this. And that I'm glad we've been able to talk and maybe each of us understands a little more about the situation.

T: Can you share with her what you understand now?

(Client expresses clarity and personal truth at the moment.)

C: Yeah. (in softer, deeper voice) I understand now a little more that you were doing what you had to do. You did the best that you could, and I guess you really don't hold anything against me. And, I guess you felt that I was doing as good as I could do. . . .

(Client's statements indicate that he is not ready to say goodbye. Therapist suggests recognition and affirmation of the work that still needs to be done.)

T: I'd like you to just consider for a moment what you can now do for yourself based on this, and share that with her—how you can ground this work and make it easier for yourself, accept this more . . . how you can do that, and perhaps what you still need to do.

C: Well, I am pleased that I'm able to do as much as I have done, the changing that I am doing now and that I have done in the last year. And I know that I did a lot better because of the changes that I've made. (Client is clear that he has not yet allowed his daughter to die.) And with you, Kathy, I intend to keep working for more openness and . . . so that I can see a little better where you were coming from. (Client indicates that some integration may be taking place.) And accept that you didn't hold anything against me. I like that. I like that a lot. . . .

T: Okay, take a minute and see if there is anything else that you want to do before we stop.

(Client indicates closure for this session with more work to do later. He experiences unblocked energy as relief.)

C: (pause) No, I think that's all I can do . . . (sigh) . . . I feel quite a lot of relief. . . .

End of Session

SUMMARY STATEMENT

This session demonstrates quite clearly the steps in the gestalt therapeutic process as they were discussed in chapter 5. Most of the session is taken up with the steps of expression and differentiation. Near the end, however, Ken affirms himself and his daughter, and he chooses to see each of them as doing the best they could. At this point, some integration of his past polarizations takes place.

After enough expression had taken place to determine where the work would focus, the techniques of dialogue and role reversal were used. These techniques allowed Ken to express and to see his daughter's point of view. He was able to release and express blocked feelings, and considerable clarity was achieved. Ken did not accept or agree with his daughter's perspective, but he was achieving clarity about it. At this point, an impasse developed: Ken was not willing to choose to let go of his gestalt of the situation.

As a possible way to get through the impasse, the therapist suggested that Ken shift to identify with the part of himself that was objective and loving. This experiment enabled Ken to disengage himself from the impasse positions, and allowed him to take substantial steps towards accepting Kathy as she was and toward letting go of his resentment.

Near the end of the session, Ken was able to affirm that he and Kathy were both doing the best they could. He was able to integrate an alienated part of himself when he said, ". . . and accept that you didn't hold anything against me. I like that. I like that a lot."

Although Ken's understanding and acceptance of Kathy's death was not complete, the process of closure had begun.

APPENDIX B:
GESTALT EXPLORATION

(The client is a young male professional counselor. The client and therapist had worked together for some time prior to the session reported here.)

Note: "C" is the client; "T" is the therapist.
C: Tuesday I played golf!
T: Great!

(The client had earlier worked on process of allowing himself to be less compulsive in his work habits.)

C: . . . and it seems like my typical style is to play well for a few holes and then not to play so well for a while . . . (T: Hmmmm.) . . . and that really fits for me . . . that's a real theme in my life—to do well for a while and then quit or back off.
(T: Yeah?) . . . and I am confused by that. I can do a lot of things well and I don't get too far into any one. I sort of vacillate. I like to do a lot of things, but sometimes I would like to follow through.

(The client has stated the life process he wishes to explore—the focus for the session.)

T: Is this during reflecting on a situation? That you think you'd like to have followed through a little more? Or is it something that you were aware of, for instance, while you were playing golf? Were you aware at the moment?

C: I think I ignore it at the moment, although I am honestly not . . . (pause) sure how the process works. The other day at golf, I started off in a fog almost certainly not thinking of what I was doing, relying just on my ability.

T: Oh, I see, your mind wasn't clicked in much.

C: Not much, no. If anything, I was a little anxious wondering how I'll play. And I play really well for a while and then I sort of switch into this other mode where . . . I'm not sure what the switch is . . .

T: You become aware of what you're doing?

(T is making suggestions that may help client to focus.)

C: Yes! That's almost exactly what happens . . . almost exactly right . . . I start thinking about it and then . . . well, it's like switching into a middle ground where I think about it a little bit and then I switch into a mode . . . Like the other night I played well and then I didn't play well at all. (T: Hmmmm.) Then I got to a point where I said, Okay! And I really concentrated and could do the things that I could really do well. I really focused, is what I did, and I started to play really well again.

T: It seems as if you have three mental states that you go into, doesn't it?

C: Yeah . . . in a way . . . (slowly and thoughtfully) . . . (The client ignores the therapist's suggestion and goes on into something else.) Another example that I was thinking about was connected to the tension that I have felt. Like this week I have had a lot of tension . . . (T: Yes, umhmmm.) a lot of tension in my neck.

T: Did you feel that before you went back to work this week?

C: Yes, all through my vacation. (T: Uh huh.) What I am aware of in my process with that is when I take the time to do the progressive relaxation exercises I notice improvement.

T: More relaxation you mean . . .

C: Since Tuesday I have felt less tension. I have a real progressive quality. I'll feel it here (pointing) and then here (pointing) and if I don't pay any attention I'll end up with a headache.

T: As if something is trying to get your attention?

C: Yeah, yeah . . . The amazing part to me is that I don't follow through with any change. I'll feel better for a few days, I'll take 5 or 10 minutes at work for relaxing. Just sort of concentrating on my body. If I do this I really notice that it'll improve and then I'll stop doing it.

T: What's the *it*?

C: The tension, it'll improve, but I'll stop doing exercises for a few days and the tension will be back.

T: Well, I was thinking about this in terms of the states you experience in playing golf. (C: Yeah . . .) There is a kind of an equation here, isn't there?

C: Yes, I think so. I'm not clear though.

T: The word that came to my mind was *discipline*. There's a state where you don't need any, or it comes easy, and it isn't even like discipline

because you're making choices and that process works fine. Then . . .
I don't know . . . (C: Yeah.) it's like something slips, as in those middle
holes in your golf game. But then you pick up and become . . . I don't
know if *disciplined* is the right word . . .

C: (animated) Oh, yes, it fits. I've thought about discipline a whole lot,
as in follow through. And that fits into *every area of my life* . . . at least
that's my interpretation of it. I get something started and have a hard
time finishing it. That happens all the time. (T: Yeah.) All the time!

*(The expression stage of the session is completed. The client has experienced the
focused-upon process clearly. The therapist now turns to an in-depth exploration
of the golf-game experience.)*

T: Can you put yourself back there on the golf course so that we can
see if we can get any more clarity about what happens at the point
where something slips?

C: Yeah, let me see if I can get back there . . . (closes eyes and long
pause follows) Let's see . . . going out to the first hole I am aware of
feeling kind of nervous about how I will perform . . . Uh . . . I think
that I just want to go out and have fun and on the other hand I need
to play well . . . And so I go up to the first tee and it's almost like I
have absolutely no idea what's going to happen. And I hit a tremendous shot and I feel a lot of relief . . . and . . . as I walk down the
fairway I feel good and then I feel some pressure that the second shot
needs to be *very* good . . . and . . . I shoot and it's okay, just okay.
And, let's see . . . . I think, wouldn't it be nice if I could par these holes
. . . (pause)

T: (softly) You do well on the second hole . . .

C: Well, I didn't do as well as I might on the second hole. And on the
third and fourth I made bad shots and I remember thinking, well of
course they're bad shots. I didn't even focus on what I wanted to do
. . . Sort of like a random feeling . . . (T: Um hmmm.) So I play along
and I hit some good shots and some poor shots and some okay shots.
But at some point I think, okay you gotta start playing smart here. So
I chose a specific club and I hit better, and the rest of the way I played
pretty well. (opens eyes and looks at therapist)

T: Well, I remember your thinking on the second hole that it'd be nice
if you could par these holes. What I thought was that you've introduced the possibility that you might not play well. (C: Um hmmm.)
That's not how you phrased it in your mind.

C: I see what you're saying.

T: Maybe something like, wouldn't it be nice but I know I'm not going
to?

C: Hmmm. Yeah . . . That's really interesting. What it brings up for
me is that it's really hard to stay focused on one shot. Whether or not
I shoot par for the whole round, I know what the chances are and
they're not good.

T: And then your concentration is diluted . . .

C: And I can't see each shot. That's what it feels like . . . I'm always
thinking of these other things and can't focus on what I'm doing . . .
I want to impress people because I am good . . .

T: But you don't because something happens on the second hole to prevent it. Until down at the fifth or sixth, somewhere down there you think, all right now! or okay now! to yourself.

C: Yeah. Yeah.

(At this point the client and therapist explore other experiences in which he is prevented from performing at his best until the therapist reports a figural awareness.)

T: Something just occurs to me. I don't know if it fits. I was thinking about that experience in golf . . . about the second and third holes . . . about you thinking, wouldn't it be good if I could par these. . . . What occurred to me was that maybe at the time you think that thought you are focused outside yourself. You just said something about pleasing others . . .

C: Oh, yeah!

T: . . . and wanting to look good. Maybe losing the *discipline*, the focusing inward is what happens.

C: Absolutely! Absolutely! And that's the same as it feels physically. It's like I want to ignore what's going on internally and I pay attention to all the cues out there that may question, and I *won't* take the time to go inside to the confidence. It's the same as when I have a presentation to give. It's like doing research in general. It takes a lot of discipline. Writing itself takes a lot of discipline. I have a really hard time with that. (T: Hmmmm.) The best writing I do is when I have put off and the deadline is there and I just . . . blaaah . . . do it! And the stuff I write will be *good*.

T: When the deadline is there that's the point when you say, All right, David! You've gotta do it!

C: Yeah, at that time there's no choice. I have to turn something in and I do. (T: Ah.) At that time I *choose* to do it. Before that I *choose* not to. *(The client is animatedly exploring one aspect of what blocks him from performing well.)*

T: Well, you *don't* and then you *do*. But in golf it's not like that, right?

C: I'm not sure. That's a good question. In other situations I think what I do is avoid it.

T: What's the *it*?

C: Avoid completing it. Avoid doing it.

T: Avoid focusing?

C: In some cases that would be true.

(The client explores avoidance; he has pointed to an impasse. The client continues to explore what comes into his mind as examples of blocking.)

C: (continues) A couple of job candidates came in this year and each made a presentation. And I thought each *had* a presentation and they really put themselves out there . . . almost like actors on stage . . .

T: (slowly) On stage . . .

C: And I thought, Oh man, I'd *really* like to be able to do that. I'd be more likely to say, Let's talk, rather than make a real presentation.

T: Yes, I see that. That's what you are doing with your students.

C: Yeah, and there's a lot of quality in that, but I'd like to be able to do both!

T: Oh, yes. This is not an either-or, David. It's a both-and. This is really important. A lot of presenters can't lead discussions worth a damn. Both capabilities are really important!

C: Exactly! Yesterday in group we were talking something about this. Someone said that it made him extremely nervous to get up in front of 300 people. It doesn't make him nervous to present in front of 10. And I said, It's exactly the opposite with me. I can present before 300 easily. I don't care much about 300 people. But with 10 . . . (T: Hmmmm.) That's really interesting . . . I'm not sure why that is.

T: I *think* it has to do with . . . I'm not sure I have the right words . . . but with 300 people you get *very little* feedback. You know, you present, and there's a break . . . (C: True.) . . . and once in a while you get a little talk. (C: True.) But with 10 people you're bound to interact. You're much closer . . . and if you're a certain kind of person, that could be bothersome . . .

C: Yeah, I think I'm good at facilitating other people but I'm not good at putting myself out there with people I know. You understand what I'm saying?

(The client is making a more cogent statement as to the blockage.)

T: Yes, definitely. It seems to me that these are just different capabilities. I think it'd be good for you to develop the capability of putting yourself out in situations you know.

C: I *do* agree with that. To a degree. (pause) What I get nervous about in the small group is when I am put into the role of "expert."

T: Oh, yes.

C: In the small group, I am more likely to do a processing thing. I found out a couple of semesters ago that I really like to do that kind of facilitation with small groups of students. I really like it a lot. Really a *lot*. (T: Um hmmmm.) And in that situation the *expert* role is fairly comfortable for me. (T: Okay.) And I could still do the process stuff. Uh . . . it's harder for me to be the expert with students who are farther along in school—have completed their Masters, for example. And it's harder yet for me to do it with colleagues.

T: Check what assumptions you are making, David. I hear you making some assumptions about their expertise.

C: (long silence) What do you hear?

T: I hear that you assume that they may be expert enough to perhaps wipe you out when you present something.

C: (immediately) Absolutely! (both laugh) Yeah! And in writing—to put down my ideas and to send them out there is like . . . it seems so hard that it's easier to avoid doing it. I do that!

T: I really *do* understand what you're talking about. . . . There may be a safe way—not to say anything—but . . .

C: Yeah! That really fits! Yes, I see that in my work. And I think that same principle applies in these other parts of my life.

T: Yes, I was thinking about that.

C: What I do is I think I have got to be really good. And that just gets my head going thinking about a lot of other things—other than what I am involved in.

T: Yes.

C: And I know that I could be good at a lot of things in my life . . . if I could put my mind to the doing of them.

T: Like what you said about golf, All right, David! (both laugh)

C: Right! That's right!

T: It's focusing at the moment, whereas you are very diffuse before that.

C: That's right. Somewhere in that diffusion I'm looking for excuses . . . it's the same old thing.

T: The same old thing about being perfect so that no one can be critical.

C: Right!

(The client has reached a point of clarity about the blockage.)

T: (jokingly) Everything you do has got to be perfect! Just perfect, David!

C: Right! Right! It keeps me from starting jobs . . . working on my car . . . I can think of a million reasons . . . (T: Sure.) But the real reason is that I'm not sure what's going to happen, if I can do the job. So it takes ten times longer to do a project . . . two days to sort of stew and fret about it . . . even house projects . . . (T: Yes.) It just consumes so much energy.

T: I believe you. I can see it.

C: Yes, I see it too.

T: You know what comes to mind, David.

(The therapist suggests a possible way out of the impasse by setting up hypotheses during which the client follows his own line of thought. He speaks slowly and pauses often.)

T: I just had an image. I had a sense of a part of you back of you, maybe standing on your shoulders . . . maybe this ties in with tense shoulders . . . a part that stands there and says, "Now, you've got to do this *perfectly!*" As compared to you being here as you are in the chair saying, "Now, I'm going to give this my best shot . . . ,"

C: Yeah, that fits. (pause) That definitely fits. I think of sports scenes like golf or basketball . . .

T: Yes, you use your body . . .

C: I can see being aware of thinking. Well, you make it or you don't make it, you do your best. You're not doing so hot anyway, so what do you have to lose??

T: Yes . . .

C: (long pause) Expectations have a lot to do with this scene.

(The client has reached another point of clarity.)

T: Sure.

C: I think I like to have expectations, and on the other hand I see how much trouble it causes.

T: I do know. I am not sure we can ever be without expectations . . .

but I have a friend who is trying. She wants to let go of completed images of the future in favor of a sense of expectancy. (C: Hmmmm.) That's a great project. But I am not sure that those of us who have spent so many years using our cognitive processes as we have can ever let go of the cognitions and expectations. But we *can* quit investing in them.

C: Yeah . . . yeah. Um hmmm. I am just aware of how I scare myself with my expectations. Especially in the last couple of years. A good example is at my Dad's wedding recently.

T: Right. You mentioned that last time.

C: I felt real scared . . . almost a panic attack about . . . "What if I faint??!" That's been a real fear . . . Yes, all this thinking . . . Forward . . . forward . . . forward stuff . . . maybe's about the future.

T: Yes.

C: As I was approaching the wedding I was thinking reasons why I might not perform as I should . . . what will people think of me . . . it's almost like what will people think if I'm nervous, or if I don't say or do the right things. I spent several days just being nervous (T: Um hmmm.) I had picked up a book about panic attacks that had a lot of suggestions mostly about staying in the moment.

T: Well, panic attacks happen when you are way out ahead in your mind of where you are really.

C: Exactly! So before the wedding, I spent some time relaxing and imagining the parts of the wedding as they might happen easily. I can't say that I wasn't nervous but I didn't feel that I just couldn't do this. The imagery kept me just going through, and I managed.

T: Good!

C: This business of being here now is so difficult. All the expectations . . . But when I thought ahead *realistically*, the thinking made things easier . . . realistically rather than catastrophizing everything. My mind catastrophizes *constantly*. This may happen or this terrible thing . . . or this . . . *constantly*.

(The client makes a further clear statement regarding the blockage.)

T: Yes. Yes.

C: All of those expectations bad. Instead of keeping the thoughts in a positive frame.

T: Or even a neutral one . . . (C: Yes.) You see? (C: Yes!) A positive frame says what's going to happen will be all right. A neutral frame says, "Well, I don't know what's going to happen" . . . (C: Yeah.) Well, this seems clear, David.

C: Yes, it is clear. But let me test this. It seems like I know all that.

T: (chuckles) Yes, I don't think we have uncovered anything entirely new.

C: For example, I know that when I practice relaxation I feel better. And I don't practice! It's really amazing to me, but I don't.

(The client has arrived back at the point at which the session started but with a depth of understanding that is new. The therapist decides to suggest another kind of experiment: the exploration of the difference between the client as he is in the

therapy session and as he is elsewhere. What emerges is that the client feels dependent on the therapist while the therapist does not experience him in that way at all.)

T: (concluding exploration) . . . and I've never felt that kind of experience in you. But maybe you haven't clarified that in yourself.

C: Yeah . . . Really . . . I flash on a lot of scenes . . . I like team sports rather than other kinds . . . It's very difficult for me to take center stage . . .

T: But, see, you can! And other people see you doing that. That's the alternative route that we're exploring.

C: Yes. (pause) That's an intriguing one. (pause) I do think, on the one hand, that I can do a lot of things . . .

T: Do you *really* now? Say that again.

C: What we are saying is *can*. Right?

T: Yes. Not do you want to but *can* you. Okay?

C: I really think I can. I really think I can. And I don't know what stops me. But I really think I can do many things very well.

(The client begins the closure section of the session. Although he dilutes the experience, his focus is on the positive rather than the blockage.)

T: If you really think that you can, then we need to look at what opportunities you may have. I don't know what statement you want to make.

C: Yes, what is the statement I want to make? . . . Maybe, "Okay, David, you can do it on your own and it doesn't matter what other people think about it."

T: Right!

C: That's what it's really about. Both of those are at issue—that I can do it on my own *and* that it doesn't matter what others think.

T: I believe that.

C: In some cases I do believe I can perform on my own, like golf. I *know* I can play golf. Yet I worry so much about it.

T: That doesn't sound like real worry to me. It sounds more like losing the focused attention that it takes to play golf.

C: But I worry also about what the other guys will think of me.

T: Let's bring the reality into this. Who are these guys?

C: They are two very good friends.

T: One of them is going to give you a bad time if you blow it?

C: No!

T: Don't you see that this is another example of this thing in your mind that gets ahead of you? If you look at the reality, another picture, a very different picture, comes clear.

C: Yeah, it really is. It really is.

T: (long pause) It's powerful too, David. It really is. The focus in our minds is really powerful and profound in what is does to us. (C: Yeah . . .) For good or ill . . .

C: That's what *being here now* says to me—don't think about it . . . do it! Just do it! So I think, Why don't I follow through??

T: But that's the wrong response, David. See? *Why* questions lead you

down the other path into your mind. All they do is prevent you from
doing.

C: Okay. (voice animated) Where that leaves me . . . let me summarize
this . . . is again back to making choices.

*(The client now proceeds to explore difficulties in making choices—too many
options, too many thoughts about them.)*

C: I can remember the days that I have felt good . . . when I have just
sat down and done things.

T: Of course.

C: And I think that I really have accomplished a lot. I *know* it. And I
feel great.

T: You know, David, that we have gotten closer to the core of what you
and I have been working on all along than we ever have. Do you experience that too?

C: Yes, although I don't have it pinned down.

T: I don't know what we might do to clarify.

C: I keep coming back to the word *choices*. Once I make a choice I can
see clearly what I need to do. (T: Yes.) I really do want to follow through
. . . (T: Yes.) and before that I must decide what I really want to do.
Where to put that energy. (T: Hmmmm.) Seems harder to decide for
some reason.

T: Maybe that's where the perfection thing comes in. The question may
be which of these is *best*, instead of which comes *first*.

C: (long pause) What comes to mind is that if I choose this, then I won't
be able to do that. (pause) Or if I choose this, then I may disappoint
someone or someone may be upset . . . and another part is that if I
choose this, then I truly won't be able to do that which I really also
want to do.

T: Instead of thinking, this now and that later.

C: Yes, I want it all now or none of it now. (laughter)

T: But you know that all of the things you fear have happened to you.
Haven't they? You have been disagreed with . . . your wife has been
upset with you . . .

C: I don't like it.

T: But it has happened, hasn't it?

C: Yeah, that's right.

T: It's like you don't do things because you are afraid of things that
have already happened to you. And that you've survived! (pause) Of
course we don't expect our responses to be rational. (both laugh)

C: You know, I have been doing what I want to do more lately. I told
my wife what I wanted, and we worked things out just fine. But you
know I really do want to do all of the things that sit around on my
desk.

T: I really do understand what you say. You see my desk. And the piles
of books, all of which I want to read.

C: Well, what do *you* do about that?

T: The main thing that comes to mind is that I gave up timing everything in my mind. Now when I sit down, a certain book will hop out
at me or a certain piece of work emerges clear so I do it. I've had some

stuff on my desk for months, and I don't know when I'll get to it. But sometime I will. (David laughs.) I've quit worrying, you know. Because I know that whatever is important to me will get dealt with if I follow my inner process.

C: You mean really quit worrying??

T: Yes. Because there's a pretty wise part of me that knows what's important, what's needed now and what's needed next . . . and so on.

C: Yeah. What popped into my mind was *discipline* again. It doesn't matter what I choose to do . . . it matters that I do it.

T: Damn right! Did you hear what you just said?

C: Yes. I did.

T: Say that again. That's sounds like a rule of life, David.

C: (slowly) It doesn't matter which I do, it matters that I do it. (pause) Yeah. That's so true. And I think and think and nothing. . .

T: Yes. Thinking takes the edge off of doing, takes the energy that could be used in the doing. (C: Hmmmm.) And the gestalt is never really finished. I never get the freedom that comes with the contact of *doing*.

C: As opposed to what I'm supposed to do . . . (pause for good eye contact between client and therapist) This seems to be a good place to stop.

T: I agree.

End of Session

SUMMARY STATEMENT

This session illustrates the kind of interaction that follows a dialogic pattern. Some possibilities for a classic differentiation process approach appeared (as the thinking vs doing polarity or the presenting self vs facilitation of others polarity); however, the client mentioned needing to talk and the therapist judged that the client's process would have been interrupted deleteriously if a classic self-dialogue experiment had been suggested. None of the material that emerged in the session was new, as David pointed out. However, his personal intense involvement in the experiences was quite different from that in earlier sessions. The pauses for reflection were full of energy. The statements concluding each section of the exploration were authentic: "I get something started and have a hard time finishing it," "I'm good at facilitating other people but I'm not good at putting myself out there with people I know," "My mind catastrophizes constantly" are exemplary. David is working to loosen the I-boundary to allow more self-expression; he is confronting the perfectionism and irrational fear of criticism that keep him blocked at the impasse point.

The therapist both follows and leads in the dialogue. The leading statements are offered as suggestions, usually using the "let me feed you a line" format. That is, the therapist shares the ideas and images that come to mind, even though no groundwork may have been laid for them. In this case, the client and therapist know each other well and have worked together for some time. The fact that the client is a fellow professional makes it possible for the therapist to use professional language and to be ruthless in the interaction, although in a gentle way.

It should be noted that the subsequent session David did a classic piece of work that further clarified the discriminations that emerged in this session.

References

Aylward, J. (1988). A session with Cindy. *The Gestalt Journal, 11,* 51–62.

Bandler, R., & Grinder, J. (1975). *The structure of magic.* Palo Alto, Calif.: Science and Behavior Books.

Bandura, A. (1977). *Social learning theory.* Englewood Cliffs, N.J.: Prentice-Hall.

Berger, P.L., Berger, B., & Kellner, H. (1973). *The homeless mind: Modernization and consciousness.* New York: Random House.

Beisser, A. (1970). The paradoxical theory of change. In J. Fagan & I.L. Shepherd (Eds.), *Gestalt therapy now* (pp. 77–80). New York: Harper & Row.

Boulding, K.E. (1956). *The image.* Ann Arbor, MI: The University of Michigan Press.

Brown, G. (1986). *The neurotic behavior of organizations.* Cleveland, OH: Gestalt Institute of Cleveland Press.

Brown, G., Mintz, E., Nevis, S.M., Smith, E.W.L., & Harman, R. (1987). The Training of Gestalt therapists: A symposium. *Gestalt Therapy, 10,* 73–106.

Brown, G., From, I., Latner, J., Miller, M.V., Polster, E., Polster, M., Rawle, M., Wysong, J., Yontef, G., & Zinker, J. (1988, June). Panel presentation by the editorial board of *The Gestalt Journal.* Symposium presented at the meeting of the annual conference on the Theory and Practice of Gestalt Therapy, Montreal.

Brown, J.R. (1978). Ritual and Gestalt: The gestalt group in high relief. *The Gestalt Journal, 1,* 68–74.

Buber, M. (1958). *I and thou* (2nd ed.). New York: Charles Scribner & Sons.

Bugental, J.F.T. (1965). *The search for authenticity.* New York: Holt, Rinehart & Winston.

Cannon, W.B. (1963). *The wisdom of the body.* New York: W.W. Norton.

Cassirer, E. (1953). *Language and myth* (S.K. Langer, Trans.). New York: Dover Publications. (Original work published 1946).

Cohen, R.C. (1970). Therapy in groups: Psychoanalytic, experiential, and Gestalt. In J. Fagan & I.L Shepherd (Eds.), *Gestalt therapy now* (pp. 130–139). New York: Harper & Row.

Combs, A.W., Richards, A., & Richards, F. (1975). *Perceptual psychology.* New York: Harper & Row.

Combs, A.W. & Snygg, D. (1959). *Individual behavior* (2nd ed.). New York: Harper & Row.

Coopersmith, S. (1967). *The antecedents of self-esteem.* San Francisco: Freeman.

Coopersmith, S., & Feldman, R. (1974). Fostering a positive self-concept and high self-esteem in the classroom. In R.H. Coop & K. White (Eds.), *Psychological concepts in the classroom* (pp. 192–225). New York: Harper & Row.

Denner, B. (1970). Deception, decision making, and Gestalt therapy. In J. Fagan & I.L Shepherd (Eds.), *Gestalt therapy now* (pp. 301–309). New York: Harper & Row.

Derman, B. (1976). The gestalt thematic approach. In E.W.L. Smith (Ed.), *The growing edge of Gestalt therapy* (pp. 151–159). New York: Brunner/Mazel.

Edie, J.M. (1964). Introduction. In M. Merleau-Ponty, *The primacy of perception* (pp. xiii–xix). Evanston, IL: Northwestern University Press.

Egan, G. (1986). *The skilled helper* (3rd ed.). Pacific Grove, CA: Brooks/Cole.

Ellis, A. (1958). Rational psychotherapy. *Journal of General Psychology, 59*, 36–49.

Enright, J.B. (1976). Thou art that: Projection and play in therapy and growth. In C. Hatcher & P. Himelstein (Eds.), *The handbook of Gestalt therapy* (pp. 469–476). New York: Jason Aronson.

Erikson, E. (1964). *Insight and responsibility*. New York: W.W. Norton.

Erikson, E. (1968). *Identity: Youth and crisis*. New York: W.W. Norton.

Fagan, J. (1970). The task of the therapist. In J. Fagan & I.L. Shepherd (Eds.), *Gestalt therapy now* (pp. 88–106). New York: Harper & Row.

Fiedler, F.E. (1950). A comparison of therapeutic relationships in psychoanalytic, nondirective, and Adlerian therapy. *Journal of Consulting Psychology, 14*, 435–436.

Frankl, V. (1963). *Man's search for meaning*. New York: Washington Square Press.

Frew, J. (1986). The functions and patterns of occurrence of contact styles during the developmental phases of the Gestalt group. *The Gestalt Journal, 9*(1), 55–70.

Gagnon, J.H. (1981). Gestalt therapy with the schizophrenic patient. *The Gestalt Journal, 4*(1), 29–46.

Gandhi, M. (1949). *The story of my experiments with truth*. London: Phoenix Press.

Gendlin, E. (1962). *Experiencing and the creation of meaning*. New York: Free Press.

Gendlin, E. (1967). Values and the process of experiencing. In A.R. Mahler (Ed.), *The goals of psychotherapy* (pp. 180–225). New York: Appleton-Century-Crofts.

Glasser, W. (1985). *Control theory*. New York: Harper & Row.

Goldstein, K. (1939). *The organism*. New York: American Book Co.

Greenwald, J.A. (1972). The ground rules in gestalt therapy. *Journal of Contemporary Psychotherapy, 5*(1), 3–120.

Guntrip, H. (1969). *Schizoid phenomena, object relations and the self*. New York: International Universities Press, Inc.

Hall, C.S., & Lindzey, G. (1978). *Theories of personality* (3rd ed.). New York: Wiley.

Harman, R. (1979). Gestalt therapy with sexually impotent males: A holistic approach. *The Gestalt Journal, 2*(2), 65–72.

Hatcher, C., & Himelstein, P. (Eds.). (1976). *The handbook of Gestalt therapy*. New York: Jason Aronson.

Hendlin, S.J. (1987). Gestalt therapy: Aspects of evolving theory and practice. *Humanistic Psychologist, 15*(3), 184–196.

Horney, K. (1945). *Our inner conflicts*. New York: W.W. Norton.

Hycner, R. (1985). Dialogical Gestalt therapy: An initial proposal. *The Gestalt Journal, 8*(1), 23–49.

Hycner, R. (1987). An interview with Erving and Miriam Polster. *The Gestalt Journal, 10*(2), 27–66.

Jacobs, L.N. (1978). I-Thou relation in Gestalt therapy (Doctoral dissertation, California School of Professional Psychology, 1978). *Dissertation Abstracts International, 40*, 3937B.

Jourard, S. (1964). *The transparent self*. Princeton, NJ: D. Van Nostrand.

Jung, C.G. (1938). *Psychology and religion*. New Haven: Yale University Press.

Kelly, E. (1962). The fully functioning self. In A.W. Combs (Ed.), *Perceiving, behaving, becoming: A new focus for education* (pp. 9–20). Washington, D.C.: Association for Supervision & Curriculum Development.

Kelly, G. (1963). *A theory of personality: The psychology of personal constructs*. New York: W.W. Norton.

Kierkegaard, S. (1967). *Soren Kierkegaard's Journals and Papers* (H.V. Hong & E.H. Hong, Trans.). Bloomington, IN: Indiana University Press. (Original works publishsed 1909–1948)

Kohler, W. (1973). *The mentality of apes* (2nd ed.) (E.Winter, Trans.). New York: Harcourt, Brace & World. (Original work published 1927)

Kohut, H. (1971). *The analysis of the self.* New York: International University Press.

Kohut, H. (1985). *Self psychology and the humanities.* New York: W.W. Norton.

Korb, M.P. (1974). *The function of language in identity formation.* Unpublished manuscript.

Korb, M.P. (1984). Therapeutic steps and processes in maturation: A Gestalt approach. *The Gestalt Journal, 7*(2), 43–59.

Korb, M.P. (1988). The numinous ground: I - Thou in gestalt work. *The Gestalt Journal, 9*(1), 97–106.

Korzybski, A. (1933). *Science and sanity.* Lakeville, CT: Institute of General Semantics.

Krause, G. (1977). *Some notes on gestalt therapy training.* Unpublished manuscript.

Lacan, J. (1975). *The language of the self: The function of language in psychoanalysis* (A. Wilden, Trans.) New York: Delta Books. (Original work published 1956)

Langer, S. (1951). *Philosophy in a new key.* New York: New American Library.

Levitsky, A., & Perls, F.S. (1970). Rules and games of gestalt therapy. In J. Fagan & I.L. Shepherd (Eds.), *Gestalt therapy now* (pp. 140–149). New York: Harper & Row.

Lewin, K. (1951). *Field theory in social science: Selected theoretical papers.* New York: Harper & Row.

Lifton, R.J. (1976). *The life of the self.* New York: Basic Books.

Lowen, A. (1967). *The betrayal of the body.* London: Collier Macmillan.

Marsh, H.W., & Shavelson, R. (1985). Self-Concept: Its multifaceted, hierarchical structure. *Educational Psychologist, 20*(3), 107–123.

Maslow, A. (1954). *Motivation and personality.* New York: Harper & Row.

Maslow, A. (1962). *Toward a psychology of being.* Princeton, NJ: Van Nostrand.

Masterson, J.F. (1985). *The real self: a developmental, self, and object relations approach.* New York: Brunner/Mazel.

May, R. (1969). *Love and will.* New York: W.W. Norton.

Merleau-Ponty, M. (1964). An unpublished text by Maurice Merleau-Ponty: A prospectus of his work (A.B. Dallery, Trans.). In J.M. Edie (Ed.), *The primacy of perception* (pp. 3–11). Evanston, IL.: Northwestern University Press.

Miller, M.V. (1988). Introduction. In F.S. Perls, *Gestalt therapy verbatim* (pp. i–xviii). Highland, NY: The Center for Gestalt Development, Inc.

Moreno, J.L. (1946). *Psychodrama.* New York: Beacon House.

Mucchielli, R. (1970). *Introduction to structural psychology.* New York: Funk & Wagnalls.

Naranjo, C. (1970). Present-centeredness: Techniques, prescriptions and ideal. In J. Fagan & I.L. Sheperd (Eds.), *Gestalt therapy now* (pp. 47–69). New York: Harper & Row.

Naranjo, C. (1976). Expressive techniques. In C. Hatcher & P. Himelstein (Eds.), *The handbook of Gestalt therapy* (pp. 281–305). New York: Jason Aronson.

Oaklander, V. (1978). *Windows to our children.* Moab, UT: Real People Press.

Orlinsky, D.E., & Howard, K.I. (1967). The good therapy hour: Experiential correlates of patients' and therapists' evaluations of therapy sessions. *Archives of General Psychiatry, 16*, 621–632.

Perls, F.S. (1947). *Ego, hunger, and aggression: The beginning of Gestalt therapy.* New York: Random House.

Perls, F.S. (1969). *Gestalt therapy verbatim.* Lafayette, Calif.: Real People Press.

Perls, F.S. (1972). *In and out the garbage pail.* New York: Bantam Books.

Perls F.S. (1973). *The Gestalt approach and eyewitness to therapy.* Palo Alto, Calif.: Science and Behavior Books, Bantam Books edition.

Perls, F.S., Hefferline, R.F., & Goodman, P. (1951). *Gestalt therapy: Excitement and growth in the human personality.* New York: Dell.

Piaget, J. (1952). *The origins of intelligence in children.* New York: W.W. Norton.

Polster, E. (1977). Remarks for the tenth anniversay issue. *The Gestalt Journal, 10*(1), 33–34.

Polster, E., & Polster, M. (1973). *Gestalt therapy integrated.* New York: Brunner/Mazel.

Polster, M. (1987). Gestalt therapy: Evolution and application. In J.K. Zeig (Ed.), *The evolution of psychotherapy.* New York: Brunner/Mazel.

Purkey, W.W. (1970). *Self-concept and school achievement.* Englewoods Cliffs, NJ: Prentice-Hall.

Reich, W. (1949). *Character-Analysis.* New York: Noonday Press.

Resnick, R.W. (1975). Chicken soup is poison. In F.D. Stephenson, *Gestalt therapy primer* (pp. 142–146). Springfield, IL: Charles C. Thomas.

Rickers-Ovsiankina, M. (1928). Die wiederaufnahme von interbrochenen handlungen. *Psychologische Forschung, 2,* 302–389.

Rogers, C.R. (1951). *Client-centered therapy: Its current practice, implications, and theory.* Boston: Houghton Mifflin.

Rogers, C.R. (1959). A theory of therapy, personality, and interpersonal relationships, as developed in a client-centered framework. In S. Koch (Ed.), *Psychology: A study of a science. 3. Formulations of the person and the social context* (pp. 184–256). New York: McGraw-Hill.

Rogers, C.R. (1969). *Freedom to learn: A view of what education might become.* Columbus, OH: Merrill.

Rolf, I.P. (1977). What is rolfing about? *Bulletin of Structural Integration, 6*(2), 1–7.

Rosenberg, M. (1979). *Conceiving the self.* New York: Basic Books.

Rosenfeld, E. (1982). An oral history of Gestalt therapy, Part One: A conversation with Laura Perls. In J. Wysong & E. Rosenfeld (Eds.), *An oral history of Gestalt therapy* (pp. 8–31). Highland, NY: The Gestalt Journal.

Shapiro, D. (1965). *Neurotic styles.* New York: Basic Books.

Shub, N. (1981). Psychotherapy in the classroom. *The Gestalt Journal, 4*(1), 47–56.

Simkin, J.S. (1976). The development of gestalt therapy. In C. Hatcher & P. Himelstein (Eds.), *The handbook of gestalt therapy* (pp. 223–233). New York: Jason Aronson.

Smith, E.W.L. (Ed.). (1976). *The growing edge of gestalt therapy.* New York: Brunner/Mazel.

Stratford, C.D., & Brallier, L.W. (1979). Gestalt therapy with profoundly disturbed persons. *The Gestalt Journal, 2*(1), 90–104.

Stryker, S. (1979). The profession: Comments from an interactionist's perspective. *Sociological Focus, 12,* 175–186.

Swanson, J. (1988). Boundary processes and boundary states: A proposed revision of the gestalt theory of boundary disturbance. *The Gestalt Journal, 9*(2), 5–24.

Suzuki, D.T. (1970). *The field of Zen.* New York: Harper & Row.

Tobin, S.A. (1982). Self disorders, Gestalt therapy and self psychology. *The Gestalt Journal, 5*(2), 3–44.

Tobin, S.A. (1985). Lacks and shortcomings in Gestalt therapy. *The Gestalt Journal, 8*(1), 65–71.

Van De Riet, V., Korb, M.P., & Gorrell, J. (1980). *Gestalt therapy: An introduction.* New York: Pergamon.

Wagner, J.W.L. (1983). Self concept: Research and educational implication. *Studies in Educational Evaluation, 9,* 239–251.

Wertheimer, M. (1945). *Productive thinking.* New York: Harper & Brothers.

Yapko, M.D. (1988). *When living hurts.* New York: Brunner/Mazel.

Yontef, G. (1971). *A review of the practice of Gestalt therapy.* Los Angeles: California State University.

Yontef, G. (1983). The self in Gestalt therapy: Reply to Tobin. *The Gestalt Journal, 6*(1), 55–70.

Zeigarnik, B. (1927). Das Behalten erledigter und unerledigter Handlungen. *Psychologische Forschung, 9,* 1–85.

Zinker, J. (1977). *Creative process in Gestalt therapy.* New York: Brunner/Mazel.

Author Index

165

Subject Index

About the Authors

Margaret P. Korb, called Pat by her friends, is director and director of training at The Gestalt Center of Gainesville, Florida, having retired in 1985 from community college instruction. She has an M.A. in English and a Ph.D. in Counselor Education from the University of Florida. Receiving a doctorate in 1975 fulfilled a promise made to herself when she received her B.A. in 1939. She has been a therapist and trainer in Gestalt therapy for eighteen years in graduate-level courses at the University of Florida and in private practice. She is particularly interested in the processes of on-going therapy and in the spiritual and healing aspects of therapeutic work. In training, she is interested in the processes by which novices may become experts and in the facilitation of those processes. She is a licensed mental health counselor in the State of Florida.

Jeffrey Gorrell received his Ph.D. in educational psychology from the University of Florida in 1975. He is Professor of Educational Psychology at Southeastern Louisiana University and also teaches counseling courses in the graduate school. Outside the university setting, he has worked extensively in areas related to community psychology, especially in crisis intervention. His current professional interests center around the personalization of knowledge and learning as well as the affective and cognitive factors in learning and experience. He recently has been a Fulbright Scholar and a research consultant with the Sri Lankan National Institute of Education. Recent research has focused on self-efficacy, cognitive modeling, significant influences that teachers have on knowledge representation, and learning via computer-simulated problem-solving.

Vernon Van De Riet received his graduate training in clinical psychology at Florida State University and completed his internship at the Judge Baker Guidance Center and Harvard University Medical Center in Boston. From 1962 to 1979, he was on the faculty of the Department of Clinical Psychology at the University of Florida, where he conducted a Gestalt therapy training program for ten years. He is a certified Gestalt therapist and has extensive training and experience in the Freudian, Rogerian, and Jungian approaches to personality and psychotherapy. He is also a certified trainer in psychosynthesis. Since 1979, Dr. Van De Riet has been director of Affiliated Psychological Services in South Pasadena, California. Along with his private practice, he conducts an on-going Gestalt therapy training program. He is a diplomate of the American Board of Psychotherapy and a member and past officer of the Gestalt Therapy Institute of Los Angeles.

Psychology Practitioner Guidebooks

Editors
Arnold P. Goldstein, Syracuse University
Leonard Krasner, Stanford University & SUNY at Stony Brook
Sol L. Garfield, Washington University in St. Louis